Get used ....

Have you found a spotless lamb for sacrifice?
–Pharisee to the Shepherd, Pilot Ep.

That's not for you.
–Jesus to Mary Magdalene, Ep. 1

I was one way and now I'm completely different.
–Mary Magdalene to Nicodemus, Ep. 2

I hope my next students ask the same questions you do.
–Jesus to the children, Ep. 3

You have much bigger things ahead of you.
–Jesus to Simon, Ep. 4

If not now, when?
–Mother Mary to Jesus, Ep. 5

Please don't turn away from me.
–Leper to Jesus, Ep. 6

Everything I thought I knew, what if it's wrong?
–Matthew to his mother, Ep. 7

It would be good if you believed me.
–Jesus to the Samaritan woman, Ep. 8

The Chosen Study
FOOD FOR THE HUNGRY

The Chosen Study
FOOD FOR THE HUNGRY

A welcoming and
Interactive experience for everyone:
observers... skeptics... learners... seekers... followers.

The Jesus Study Team

Bill & Teresa Syrios, Dietrich Gruen,
Tori Foss, Dave Hawkins and Don & Cathy Baker

JesusStudy.org
*Watch > Discover > Relate
the Most Audacious
Story ever told.*

Do not work for the food that perishes, but for the food that endures to eternal life, which the Son of Man will give to you…. I am the bread of life whoever comes to me shall not hunger.
-Jesus (John 6:27. 35)

Crossover Press

©2023 Food for the Hungry: The Chosen Study, Season Three
(Ten Studies Inspired by The Chosen)
Bill Syrios & TJS Team

The Jesus Study and their guides are not
affiliated with *The Chosen* TV show or *Angel Studios*.

ISBN: 978-0-9716683-7-9

"The Chosen is a television drama based on the life of Jesus Christ, created, directed and co-written by American filmmaker, Dallas Jenkins. It is the first multi-season series about the life of Christ, and season one was the highest crowd-funded TV series or film project of all time.

The series' creators stated that they had hoped to distinguish the new series from previous portrayals of Jesus by crafting a multi-season, episode-based story. The series portrays Jesus 'through the eyes of those who met him.'"   –*The Chosen*, Wikipedia

The Chosen Study focuses on *filling out* the series with Scripture passages to take everyone deeper. The guide can profitably be used by individuals with the hope that they… we… facilitate outreach and learning with others in one-on-one and group contexts. After all: *People must know!*

Contents

Welcome to The Chosen Study, Season Three 8

Study and Discussion Format 10

A Word as We Begin 17

The Studies / Discussions

Study #1: Beyond Mountains & Homecoming, Ep. 8B & Ep. 1A . . 21
Micah 5:2-5; Is. 9:2-7, 35:3-6; Luke 2:1-21

Study #2: Homecoming, Episode 1 33
Luke 7:36-50

Study #3: Two by Two, Episode 2 43
Genesis 1:1-2:3; Exodus 2:8-11

Study #4: Physician, Heal Yourself, Episode 3 55
Psalm 63; Matthew: 19;13-15, 18:1-6

Study #5: Clean, Part 1, Episode 4 65
Luke 4:38-5:11

Study #6: Clean, Part 2, Episode 5 75
Luke 2:40-52; John 2:1-12

Study #7: Intensity in Tent City, Episode 6 87
Isaiah 40:3-5; Mark 1:40-2:12

Study #8: Ears to Hear, Episode 7 97
Numbers 21:4-9; John 3:14-15; 1-21

Study #9: Sustenance, Episode 8A 109
John 4:1-26

Study #10: Rest for the Weary, Episode 8B 119
John 4:27-39; Review; Looking Ahead

Your Faith Journey 127

Background Notes 133

Leader's Notes 143

Study and Leadership Resources 155

Welcome to The Chosen Study: Season Three

Like the man himself, the accounts of Jesus' life and ministry are unique in the field of literature. Ancient writings include historical accounts, personal memoirs, and mythological stories. But none of these styles describe how Matthew, Mark, Luke, and John wrote.

They combine the roles of historian, biographer, theologian, and pastor. These "reporters" are not simply neutral observers but men who had been deeply influenced by the message they desired to communicate. Lacking literary precedent, second-century Christians called them *Evangelists,* and their writings, *The Gospels*.

The English word "gospel" comes from the Greek term, *evangelion,* which means "good news." The four Evangelists wanted their readers to not only know how remarkable Jesus was, but to know how good his message becomes in the lives of those who embrace it.

To understand that message better, we have selected key Bible passages portrayed in *The Chosen*. So, wherever you may be spiritually— an **observer... skeptic... learner... seeker... or follower**—we are glad you've joined us to learn from those who knew Jesus best.

Bible Study 2.0 = Food + Film + Scripture + Discussion

The Chosen Study includes ten studies. We typically:

–*Choose your study* from *The Chosen* or *The Bible Series* (pp. 156-157).

–*Meet weekly* to watch>discover>relate and to develop friendships.

–*Start with a meal*, potluck, or finger food to relax with each other.

–*Have no need* to bring Bibles. This guide includes the Scripture used.

–*Share* at our comfort level. No one is asked to sing, pray or read aloud.

–*Are facilitated* by a leader who guides group discussion and pace.

The Chosen & Bible Series from The Jesus Study

Our purpose is to equip followers to facilitate vibrant, *evangelizing, discipleship communities* that draw people in to watch, discover and relate to Jesus. *How can we serve you?* For Resources: pages 155-163.

Size Options: How large is your group? (See also page 146.)

One-on-One
Get-Togethers   or

Small Group
Meetings   or

Small/Large (8+)
Group Gatherings

Time Options: How much time do you have?

Longer: WATCH > DISCOVER > RELATE with food, as set out in this guide, takes *2½ to 3 hours*. **This format is most impactful and cited below.** *

Medium: If limited to *1½ to 2 hours*, you will need to skip questions or just study the first Discover section to condense and keep up the pace.

Shorter: If the group has less time, say *an hour*, you could: 1) watch the episode and, 2) study the passages before coming. Then as you meet, you would discuss what you watched / studied in preparation. (This option is less than ideal if members' preparation is inconsistent.)

*EXAMPLE: Midweek Evening	*EXAMPLE: Saturday Morning
5:45 ARRIVE: 15 min. to gather	**8:45 ARRIVE:** 15 min. to gather
6:00 POTLUCK: 30 min. relax/eat	**9:00 LITE BREAKFAST:** 15 min.
6:30-8:45 *THE CHOSEN STUDY*	**9:15-11:30 *THE CHOSEN STUDY***

Where to Meet

Churches are convenient, accessible, and often free, with kitchens and tables. Also, look for non-church, friendly alternatives such as hotel conference or community rooms, homes, colleges, offices, and cafés.

GUIDE OVERVIEW: 3-Step Process ➡ Drive it HOME

The Chosen Study guide provides a means of bringing people together to study and discuss Chosen episodes with Scripture. This framework gives direction to dynamic group studies and discussions:

PRIOR To STUDY How to Lead the Study

Tips to help current (and future) leaders prepare. Please read pages 18-19 fully.

1 { WATCH View Episode Together **FROM The CHOSEN**

Questions that take us deeper into

2 { DISCOVER Read Passage > Mark It Up > Discuss **FROM The BIBLE**

Intro/"Look Fors"/Questions to grasp meaning.

3 {

RELATE Apply Insights to God / Life / Yourself > Discuss

Applications and summarize in a T-Shirt Design.

T-Shirt Design **Summarize study in a slogan**

The Chosen is big on merch—as are we, except ours is on paper. Crystallize your thoughts in a slogan or pick your favorite line from the show—draw it and share it!

A F T E R   S T U D Y

GUIDE COMMENTARY & FOLLOW-UP After Study

NOTES On The Study **Commentary and Historical Context**

The biblical passages' context and meaning put into perspective.

REALISTIC *That's plausible but did it happen?*

But REAL? The Chosen's artistic license put into perspective.

Drive it HOME **Review & Respond: Worship, Journaling, Prayer**

Video Insights *Further insights from selected videos*

Don't use this as a Study Guide, but as a SCRATCH PAD!

What do you think about when you hear the word "study"? Yeah, thought so. It's bad. Well, how about when you hear the term, "Mark It Up"? Not so bad, right?

Think of a Mark-It-Up study format as the *adult version of drawing with crayons.*

When young children use crayons, they don't care about much except enjoying the process. That's the idea! Be like a kid. (We'll talk about this more in Study #4!) Just swap crayons for a four-color BIC pen!

We learn through our five senses, like hearing something read aloud. So, plan on having someone who reads well read the passages.

In marking up the Scripture passage, we also use another sense that we would otherwise not: the *sense of touch*. And if we do so colorfully (enter the four-color BIC pen—very inexpensive in a 12-pack from Amazon), we add just a bit more to the learning process through the *sense of sight*. **(For more mark-it-up study, see Journaling NT, p. 158.)**

And don't worry about "drawing within the lines" or "color coding." Even if you tried, you just can't mess up this format. There's no right and wrong, there's just engagement. Hands on...literally.

So, think of this guide as a

SCRATCH PAD.

Apply the M-I-U format and have fun with it.

Yes, exactly like you did drawing those

childhood masterpieces!

1) WATCH > 2) DISCOVER > 3) RELATE ➡ Drive it HOME

1) WATCH **View Episode 1 Together** (54 min.) **> Discuss**

Example from Study #2, Episode One:
I Have Called You by Name **On next page** ➡

2) DISCOVER _Read Text > Mark It Up > Discuss_

Example from Study #2, Jesus, Simon, Woman: Lk. 7:36–50

Ask the "W" Questions

WHO is involved | **WHEN** did it happen | **WHERE** is it happening
WHAT is taking place | **HOW** is it happening... and then ask...
WHY questions to uncover the author's original meaning.

*The **"Look For"** at the end of each **INTRO** provides initial direction.

**Mark Up the passage(s) by
using a four-colored BIC pen to draw:** **On next page** ➡

–Shapes around people or places.
–Boxes around whatever you'd like.
–Lines under key words and phrases.
–Clouds wherever you'd feel like it.
–Identify change of scene, watch for
  contrast, repetition, key words.
–Write notes **On page 14** ➡

3) RELATE _Apply to God & Life_ | _After Study_: Drive it HOME

Express Your Thoughts:
Write / discuss / live out
applications from the
passages in your life—
your relationship with
God, with others, your
values, priorities, goals.

How to WATCH The Chosen

Go to <u>thechosen.tv</u> under the "Watch" tab. For the app, see <u>thechosen.tv/app</u> or search *The Chosen* in your Apple/Android app store. From the app, you can stream it to your TV or you can find *the series* on providers like Angel Studios and Amazon.

The Chosen

Always **turn on** the **TV's closed captions** to better follow the narrative. **Darken** *the room* to enhance the action. A big TV also helps!

Note: We identify the length of each episode (from 19 to 53 minutes, excluding credits) in the WATCH sections to help you pace the study. Better to leave things unsaid than to bog down.7c3x226

How to DISCOVER *a passage's meaning*

Example from LUKE 7: ³⁶ One of Pharisees asked Jesus to eat with him,

To check Jesus out

and he went into the Pharisee's house and took his place at the table. ³⁷And behold, a woman of the city, who was a sinner, when she

Uninvited & Compelled

learned that he was reclining at table in the Pharisee's house, brought an alabaster flask of ointment, ³⁸and standing behind him at his feet, weeping, she began to wet his feet with her tears and wiped

Note the action words   *Inappropriate in public*

them with the hair of her head and kissed his feet and anointed them with ointment. ³⁹Now when the Pharisee who had invited him saw this, he said to himself, "If this man was a prophet, he would have known

"sort" of woman   *Inappropriate to Simon*

who and what sort of woman this is who is touching him, for she is a sinner." ⁴⁰And Jesus answering said to him, "Simon, I have something to say to you." And he answered, "Say it, Teacher."

Very deliberate personal address

How to use the guide's questions: general then specific

Unlike most Bible studies, these studies consider the fact that your group has just spent time studying (*Discover* section). So, instead of using the guide's questions first, **start with "general questions,"** like:

... Set the scene, who's involved, and what are they doing?

... What did you see (observe/notice/appreciate) in this section?

... What strikes you (surprises you/is something new to you) here?

Then, ask general follow-up questions like: ... *Any other thoughts?*

Such questions often lead to an extended back-and-forth dialogue (see page 150). That's your discussion goal. If this happens, **you do not need to use many or any of the guide's more specific questions.** So, if/when the dialogue wanes or wanders from the main points, then you can use some of the guide's **more "specific questions,"** such as:

Contrast Jesus' attitude toward sinners with that of the Pharisees. What does Jesus say are the results for those who are "born again"?

RELATE and T-Shirt Design from the passage's meaning

Use questions to help apply the text and to summarize your takeaways by creating a T-Shirt Design (see page 28) and to use as a group wrap-up.

Drive it HOME and Video Insights to go deeper and richer

Once your study ends, there is more to think about personally during the next week (maybe, on the Sabbath). Take this a chance to review, journal and pray over important insights. We suggest that you find a special place and time to schedule this as a "God-encounter thing."

Such a time allows you to express praise, embrace gratitude, plan kindnesses, and evaluate where you are giving your time, energy, and focus: *Is this what God has for you—or is there something different?*

The ***Drive it HOME*** section ends with ***Video Insights***, which provides a wide variety of resources, from music videos to word studies to Bible teaching. This will expose you and your group to other growth opportunities available. Have your phone/tablet available or access videos by going to the links at: jesusstudy.org, under *Study Options—Season Three*

LEADER'S SUMMARY—*Take note of:*

—Pages 8-16: Explanation of the study and discussion format.

—Pages 18-19: *Prior To Study* are points to consider before each study.

—Pages 143-151: See for more in-depth leader's notes.

—For supportive video descriptions of *how to facilitate a group, see:* tinyurl.com/lead-your-study and tinyurl.com/promote-your-study.

Some studies have two segments: **WATCH → DISCOVER**

Others have three: **DISCOVER → WATCH → DISCOVER**

If you are short on time, you could summarize the first passage or skip its questions, or even eliminate it altogether. Do study and discuss the second passage together. Regardless, plan on monitoring your time and pacing yourselves to leave adequate time to end with the...

RELATE → T-Shirt Design segments
to summarize, crystallize and to have fun together!

Then, encourage personal, at-home follow-up
to review and go deeper with the...

Drive it HOME → Video Insights segments.

The 3:37 min. trailer can be used for potential group members who may be interested in coming: tinyurl.com/trailer-season-three

NOTE FOR EVERYONE: We use "tinyurl.com" to create shortened URLs for you to type into your browser window to access most of the videos.

Group P.S.—Longer Options for Study #10 (Also page 127.)

Why should you consider a longer gathering for your last meeting?
and
Why bring up the last gathering before you've had your first one?

Good questions. The answers require a *big picture explanation*, so here goes: *The Chosen Study* is not meant to be a "normal Bible Study group." There certainly is nothing wrong with such studies. They're great, but they are just not what we're doing here. Our hope is to be more inclusive. (For more, see also pages 144-145.)

Our purpose centers around inviting everyone we know to join us for a study of Jesus and his message. In doing so, we seek to build enduring friendships between us, and that's how adding a day-long or weekend bonding event (at a special place!) can help us reach these goals.

Hopefully, your last gathering won't be your last meeting, but a key bonding opportunity to add fuel to the fire of momentum... for your next Chosen Study and the new group members who will join you!

Option #1: Day-Long Study #10 Event

9:00 Lite Breakfast

9:30 Study #10, pp. 118-132

12:00 Lunch

1:30 Review: Studies #1-5/Video clips

3:00 Review: Studies #6-10/Video clips

5:00 Dinner

Option #2: Weekend Study #10 Retreat

FRIDAY: Dinner

7:00 Study #10, pp. 118-132

SATURDAY: Lite Breakfast

9:00 Morning session

12:00 Saturday Lunch

1:30 Afternoon session

6:00 Saturday Dinner

7:30 Evening Session

SUNDAY: Breakfast

9:00 Morning session/End with Lunch

For more input on creating longer events, see *Leaders* on the website.

A Word as We Begin

The Chosen is meant to take you into the eyes and ears of the people who followed Jesus. We believe that if you can see Jesus through the eyes of those who met him, you can be changed and impacted in the same way they were. If we can connect you with their burdens and struggles and questions, then ideally, we can connect you to the solution, to the answer to those questions. —Dallas Jenkins

---

The Chosen Study supports these aspirations by pairing The Chosen with Old and New Testament passages to take us deeper—together!
—The Jesus Study Team

Starting a Chosen Study? Please let us know and we'll help connect with others doing so, including ourselves. Thanks!

Leader's Note: *Buy guides and four-colored BIC pens in advance.* Participants can purchase guides themselves but it's often easier if one person buys the guides (from Amazon is easiest) along with four-color BIC pens (find 6/12 BIC pen packs on Amazon). We keep the guides affordable to encourage their widespread use. To see all our guides and to order—including **volume discounts**, see: jesusstudy.org/order-guides.

Buy some extra guides for new people and those who forget to bring theirs—it will happen. **Label these as *EXTRA* on the back cover** to use for others in subsequent weeks. Feel free to charge the participants a fee for reimbursement to cover these purchases.

If someone forgets their guide and there are no extras, go to the website **to get the PDF by typing in URL:** jesusstudy.org/season-three

–Watch the episode/study the passage(s) and take notes ahead of time. Look at the *Notes* after the questions (and other commentaries, as you see fit), as well as the *Real But Realistic?* sections.

–The *Notes* are for reference, not for discussion, unless time allows.

–Always tell your group at which question to end, so they know how far to go during the study/discussion time.

–The *T-Shirt design* is meant to be drawn and shared along with the *Relate question(s)* at the end of your study (see pages 28 and 38, etc.). Have fun with it!

–Keep up the pace! Time can pass more quickly than you expect, so watch the clock, leave things unsaid, and keep moving to finish on time. (Ask your group's permission to interrupt to keep up the pace!)

–Prepare by using *Prior To Study* on page 19, and before each study.

Page 19 is the template. All other studies follow a similar pattern.

 **Leading Study #1—facilitating checklist**

–Begin *by exchanging names* and personal info. Put together a sign-up sheet. (See page 152-153 and sign-up sheet on website under *Resources*.)

–*Have members put their names on the back cover* for identification.

–*Identify your time constraints and group size.* (See pages 9 and 146.)

–*Go through the Eight Ground Rules on* page 147. Talk about signing *The* Page 147 **Challenge** of consistent attendance. We're not here to lay on guilt, but consistency serves everyone. Have fun with stressing this!

–*Talk through the study format* by going through pages 8 to 12, so that everyone has a feel for the M-I-U and the guide's overview.

–*Read or summarize the Intro and the "Look For"* on page 22 *and have a prepared volunteer read aloud the passages* (pages 22-24).

–*Give members time for personal study* using four-color BIC pens. Monitor to end study time when appropriate. **Keep up the pace!**

–*Discuss the first four passages* by asking general discussion questions, then specific ones in small/large group as time allows (see page 14).

–*Watch the episode and discuss* (page 25).

–*Have a prepped volunteer read the Intro and passage* (pages 25-27) and *give members some time for personal study* using BIC pens. Monitor group(s) to end study time when appropriate. **Keep up the pace!**

–*Discuss the passage* by asking general, then specific questions (p. 14).

–*Spend time reflecting on, writing, and sharing the Relate questions, and the T-Shirt Design* (pages 27-28). Then share these in the group.

–*Point out the Drive it HOME and Video Insights* (pages 30-31) segments for your group. Encourage a midweek (or Sabbath) review.

Leaders: What are the key things for you to focus on?

-

-

-

-

-

-

-

-

-

-

-

-

Beyond Mountains & (S. 2, Episode 8B)

Homecoming (S. 3, Episode 1) Study #1

REVIEW: Take a few minutes to skim the events and characters in Season Three on pages 22-23. (If you haven't seen the second season yet, feel free to binge watch it later!)

Looking Back on Season Two > Discuss

Episode 1: The opening scene not only sets the stage for Season Two, but it also serves as prologue for how the Gospels were written. Here we  find **John** interviewing witnesses, writing notes and musing with Jesus' mother, Mary, about how to begin his Gospel.

After Jesus encounters **Photina**, the Samaritan woman, he and his disciples visit her hometown of Sychar for two days (John 4:43). During this time, **James** and **John** till a field, and the disciples "lose" Jesus while he fixes a cart axle. Also, Photina's husband, among others, listens to Jesus tell the Parable of the Lost Sheep (Luke 15:1-7). The parable foreshadows a fascinating encounter with a "lost sheep," **Melech**, and an interesting reference to the Good Samaritan parable.

Episode 2: The disciples welcome **Philip**—a student of John the Baptist, and friend of Andrew. Now changing allegiance from John to Jesus, he seeks out his old friend, **Nathanael,** with whom he shares the good news. Nathanael (in this show, a failed architect) was despondent over a collapsed building and the loss of his career. But he finds new purpose in meeting and following the man who saw him under a fig tree.

Episode 3: No new characters, but crowds of people line up for healing. We listen in on compelling insights as the disciples, including Mother Mary, seek to understand the movement they have joined. Tensions rise as Simon and Andrew confront Matthew about his former life. But their arguments look petty as an exhausted Jesus returns, laboring as he walks through the camp to his tent.

Episode 4: Here we meet **Jesse**, permanently lame from a childhood accident, until he is healed by Jesus some 38 years later (John 5:1-9). His brother in this show, **Simon the Zealot**—trained as an assassin, but stunned to see his brother healed—rejects his zealot vows to join this new movement. Jesus increasingly "stirs up the water," coming to the attention of the Roman authorities and Jewish religious leaders.

Episode 5: The older cousin by six months, **John the Baptist** and Jesus have a sit-down conversation. **Mary Magdalene** struggles with PTSD from a close encounter with a Roman soldier and a demon-possessed man called **Legion** (real name, **Caleb**), who is delivered by Jesus. She ends up drawn back into her old lifestyle and leaves the group, who are very concerned about her disappearance. Jesus is as well, and sends Simon and Matthew to look for and, hopefully, return her.

Episode 6: Mary falls deeper into old habits, but Simon and Matthew find her and bring her back. She meets with Jesus, who is quick to extend forgiveness. The focus on love over law, and recovery over re-lapse, stands in sharp contrast to the views of the Pharisees, **Shmuel** and **Yanni**. They seek to bring Jesus to 'justice' for what they see as blasphemy, for healings and grain-eating (harvesting) on the Sabbath.

Episode 7: Jesus and his disciples prepare for an upcoming sermon to be witnessed by thousands. But that scenario appears to blow up when Roman soldiers lead Jesus away to Capernaum for questioning before **Quintus** (the Roman Praetor from Season One) and one of Caesar's cohorts, **Atticus**, who has been tailing Jesus. Andrew, despondent over John's imprisonment, leaves the group along with Philip.

They come upon the Egyptian woman, **Tamar**, and the healed paralytic—both speaking about Jesus while Jesus is wanted for questioning. The episode ends with Jesus returning and the disciples asking him to teach them how to pray in the same manner that he does. Their desire to get "the heart and the mind right" pleases Jesus.

Episode 8: We anticipate the Big Reveal, as Jesus and Matthew work together on what will be called the *Sermon on the Mount* (Matthew 5-7). Jesus comes up with just the right introduction (the Beatitudes), while the disciples busy themselves with finding and negotiating the right spot, preparing leaflets, inviting townsfolk, welcoming old friends, and parents—plus crowd control.

Thousands gather, including one who finds himself caught up in it all, **Judas (Iscariot)**. Jesus, decked out in a blue "Prince of Peace" sash, finally takes to the stage, and... (hold the drum roll, please) the long-awaited Big Reveal will now be... delivered in Season Three.

1. *Take a moment to review and respond. Then share with the group. Who were your three favorite characters in Season Two?*

   ... And how is he or she starting to be changed by getting to know Jesus as the Messiah... or not?

   —

   —

   —

WATCH **View the last 10:15 min. from Season Two, Episode 8 (from 42:25 to 52.40) > Discuss**

INTRO: Season Two ends with **Jesus** about to take center stage and deliver what will be called the *Sermon on the Mount* (Matthew 5-7). Up to this point, Jesus and **Matthew** craft just the right  sermon intro (the Beatitudes), while other disciples busy themselves with event logistics and the women fuss over what Jesus should wear. As 1000s gather, including **Judas (Iscariot)**, Jesus beholds the crowd.

2. *What do you anticipate will happen next when the curtain is pulled back on Season Three?*

Homecoming (Ep. 1) Study #1 Continued

INTRO to Season Three, Episode 1 (8:18 minutes)

INTRO: Jesus delivers the most life-altering world-changing sermon in history. One of the Twelve, **Matthew**, who earlier (Episode 8 at the end of Season Two) helped Jesus to craft the Sermon on the Mount, is now wrecked by that sermon and must face his past and reconcile with his parents.

WATCH View *Season Three, Episode 1 (1:30-9:48 min.)* **> Discuss**

4. *What struck you about the chaotic scene outside Matthew's home?*

5. *What does Mathew do as a result of what he sees and hears—from Jesus, from the Roman authorities and from his parents?*

DISCOVER *Read Aloud > Mark It Up > Discuss*

INTRO: ??

Look for ??

THE SERMON ON THE MOUNT (Beginning of the Sermon)
MATTHEW 5:1-16 (*The Beatitudes:* See Season Two, Study #10)

Christ Came to Fulfill the Law
MATTHEW 5[17] "Do not think that I have come to abolish the Law or the Prophets; I have not come to abolish them but to fulfill them. [18] For truly, I say to you, until heaven and earth pass away, not an iota, not a dot, will pass from the Law until all is accomplished. [19] Therefore whoever relaxes one of the least of these commandments and teaches others to do the same will be called least in the kingdom of heaven, but whoever does them and teaches them will be called great in the kingdom of heaven. [20] For I tell you, unless your righteousness exceeds that of the scribes and Pharisees, you will never enter the kingdom of heaven....

Build Your House on the Rock (END of The Sermon)
Matthew 7 [24] "Everyone then who hears these words of mine and does them will be like a wise man who built his house on the rock. [25] And the rain fell, and the floods came, and the winds blew and beat on that house, but it did not fall, because it had been founded on the rock. [26] And everyone who hears these words of mine and does not do them will be like a foolish man who built his house on the sand. [27] And the rain fell, and the floods came, and the winds blew and beat against that house, and it fell, and great was the fall of it."

The Authority of Jesus
[28] And when Jesus finished these sayings, the crowds were astonished at his teaching, [29] for he was teaching them as one who had authority, and not as their scribes.

--. ?

--. ?

-- ?

RELATE How It Applies to God / Life / You > Discuss

--. ?

--. ?

NOTE FOR EVERYONE: End by completing the RELATE section and designing your T-shirt. Then share them with your group. On page one under *Come and See* and below are some T-shirt sayings. Feel free to get more creative...or not with your design and share it!

After watching > discovering > relating, What slogan would you write or draw on your T-shirt?

Example concepts/quotations summarizing the film:

Speaking of broken bones. What's the story?

Sometimes you've got to stir up the water.

It's becoming real, isn't it.? Everything we prepared for.

Draft concepts for this last study:

Final design:

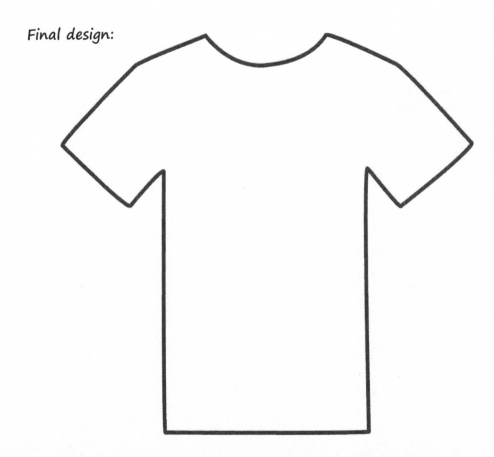

NOTES on Study #1 Commentary and Historical Context

MATTHEW 5:1-16—SERMON on the MOUNT (Beginning of Sermon)
From last Study—*The Beatitudes:* See Season Two, Study #10

-

-

Matthew 5:17-20—Christ Came to Fulfill the Law (Continue Sermon)
-

-

-

Matthew 7:24-29—Build Your House on the Rock (End of Sermon)
-

-

-

 **REALISTIC** But **REAL?**

That's plausible but did it happen?

Were Matthew's parents "tax resisters"? Was he really "dead" to them?

Many non-compliant Jews were arrested and hated, even disavowed, anyone facilitating Roman taxation. On this premise, his parents (named Alphaeus & Elisheva in this film) "sit shiva for seven days"—which is to say, their son is no more. He's dead. This sets up a future scene where Matthew, wrecked by Jesus' life-altering Sermon on the Mount, must face his past and reconcile.

At the outset, did Jesus know Judas would be a "thief" and betray him?

Judas, in this film, is a likable generous business partner (to Hadad and later Nathanael) and sibling (to Dvorah). He's a frugal steward of funds and intense (if misguided) student of Jesus. Jesus knew enough of Judas' true character to warn him of the hard choices to come. No one can worship both God and money; Jesus knew that. And Judas, reputedly a thief of funds (John 12:4-6), would learn that the hard way.

Judas' eventual betrayal of Jesus for money was not evident to his peers, but only to Jesus. Referring to Judas at the Last Supper, Jesus said, "I know those I have chosen" (John 13:18-30). This background story gives context and shows the realistic impact of the most life-altering, world-changing sermon in history. Hence, Jesus has more enemies, more notoriety, and more disciples eager to follow him anywhere.

Drive it HOME Review & Respond: Worship, Journaling, Prayer

?.

?.

?.

Video Insights: What is the Gospel? –Melissa Dougherty
Type in URL: tinyurl.com/the-gospel-defined (20:24 min.)
(Type URL exactly in your browser on device or go to website under Guides.)

Notes:

Video Insights: What is the Gospel? –Melissa Dougherty
Type in URL: tinyurl.com/the-gospel-defined (20:24 min.)
(Type URL exactly in your browser on device or go to website under Guides.)

Notes:

Getting ready for the next study.

NOTE FOR LEADERS: Begin with having new people introduce themselves.

Then, right before your group studies the passage in Luke 10 (page 36), reiterate the study process on page 10-14.

NOTE FOR EVERYONE: This guide assumes no prior preparation, but there is a place for "post-study reflection" called:

Drive it HOME

You have seen this for Study #1 on the last two pages and will see it for the next study on pages 42-43. Schedule a ***God-encounter time*** during the week to review and respond to your last study experience. We have generally included a worship video and questions to go deeper.

You also likely noted the section called:

Insight Videos

These videos are meant to give you a feel for the wide variety of available video resources. Such content provides even more biblical insight and historical context to the passages being studied.

To access them, it is necessary to be precise when typing in their URL into your computer, tablet, or phone's browser window. Our website has direct links at jesusstudy.org, under *Study Options—Season Three.*

Homecoming (Episode 1)

Study #2

INTRO: Jesus delivers the most life-altering, world-changing sermon in history. As a result, he gets more followers, more notoriety, and more enemies. **Matthew**, who earlier (Episode 8 at the end of Season Two) helped him to craft the *Sermon on the Mount*, is convicted by what he heard in the sermon and realizes he must face his past and somehow reconcile with his parents. **Joanna** (married to Chuza, Herod Antipas' household manager, who also hears the sermon) gives **Andrew** a chance to visit **John the Baptist** in prison.

WATCH **View Episode 1** (28 min., from 0:00 to 28:23) **> Discuss**

1. What stood out to you about the women funding Jesus' ministry?

2. What's Joanna's role in this? Are you suspicious of her motives? Why or why not?

3. What surprises you about the interplay of Andrew with Joanna? ... with Jesus? ... with John the Baptist?

DISCOVER Read Aloud > Mark It Up > Discuss

INTRO:

??.

Lay Up Treasures in Heaven
MATTHEW 6 [19] "Do not lay up for yourselves treasures on earth, where moth and rust destroy and where thieves break in and steal, [20] but lay up for yourselves treasures in heaven, where neither moth nor rust destroys and where thieves do not break in and steal. [21] For where your treasure is, there your heart is also.

[22] "The eye is the lamp of the body. So, if your eye is healthy, your whole body will be full of light, [23] but if your eye is bad, your whole body will be full of darkness. If then the light in you is darkness, how great is the darkness!

[24] "No one can serve two masters, for either he will hate the one and love the other, or he will be devoted to the one and despise the other. You cannot serve God and money.

Do Not Be Anxious
[25] "Therefore I tell you, do not be anxious about your life, what you will eat or what you will drink, nor about your body, what you will put on. Is not life more than food, and the body more than clothing? [26] Look at the birds of the air: they neither sow nor reap nor gather into barns,

and yet your heavenly Father feeds them. Are you not of more value than they? [27] And which of you by being anxious can add a single hour

to his span of life? [28] And why are you anxious about clothing? Consider the lilies of the field, how they grow: they neither toil nor spin, [29] yet I tell you, even Solomon in all his glory was not arrayed like one of these. [30] But if God so clothes the grass of the field, which today is alive and tomorrow is thrown into the oven, will he not much more clothe you, O you of little faith?

[31] Therefore do not be anxious, saying, 'What shall we eat?' or 'What shall we drink?' or 'What shall we wear?' [32] For the Gentiles seek after all these things, and your heavenly Father knows that you need them all. [33] But seek first the kingdom of God and his righteousness, and all these things will be added to you.

[34] "Therefore do not be anxious about tomorrow, for tomorrow will be anxious for itself. Sufficient for the day is its own trouble.

--. ?.

--. ?.

--. ?.

RELATE How It Applies to God / Life / You > Discuss

--. ?.

--. ?.

NOTE FOR EVERYONE: End by completing the RELATE questions and T-SHIRT DESIGN individually and then sharing them with your group.

After watching > discovering > relating,
What slogan would you write or draw on your T-shirt?

Draft concepts/quotations for summarizing this section:

Final design:

NOTES on Study #1 Commentary and Historical Context

PASSAGE—Title

•

•

PASSAGE—Title

•

•

•

PASSAGE—Title

•

•

•

That's plausible but did it happen?

Were women really funding Jesus' ministry and creating access to John the Baptist?

While Judas would oversee the purse and sign off on financial decisions, the real entrepreneurs—in film and Scripture—are the women. Joanna with her influential connections to Herod's court, plus Mary Magdalene with creative means (e.g., olive oil industry, reselling donated items), are shown here (see also Episodes 4 & 6). Luke 8:2-3 alludes to "many other women" supporting Jesus, such as Tamar & Ramah in this film. That Joanna arranged for Andrew to visit John the Baptist in prison is an inference from her ties to Herod, but with no record in Scripture. The women suspect Joanna of ulterior motives, but she'd be at the empty tomb and witness the Risen Christ (John 24:10).

John the Baptist is calm in prison, while Andrew is anxious on the outside. Shouldn't it be the other way around?

The film shows how the Sermon on the Mount impacts one's emotional response to all kinds of circumstances, the good with the bad.

What's with everyone kissing the door when walking out?

People are not kissing or touching the door; their kissed fingers touch the *mezuzah* posted on the doorway. Many Jewish people do this, even today, as a way of showing respect to God, much as a Catholic believer crosses himself. A *mezuzah* reminds one and all that Jewish homes are holy places and to act accordingly. A *mezuzah* is a case with a scroll in it. The scroll has two Bible texts on it. The first is Deuteronomy 6:4–9 (the *Shema,* or single-most important prayer of Jewish life), and the second is Deuteronomy 11:13–21 (which contains a most cherished blessing).

Drive it HOME Review & Respond: Worship, Journaling, Prayer

?.

?.

?.

Video Insights: What is the Gospel? –Melissa Dougherty
Type in URL: tinyurl.com/the-gospel-defined (20:24 min.)
Notes:

Video Insights: What is the Gospel? –Melissa Dougherty
Type in URL: tinyurl.com/the-gospel-defined (20:24 min.)
Notes:

NOTE TO EVERYONE: ?

Two by Two (Ep. 2)

Study #3

FROM The BIBLE

INTRO: ?

DISCOVER **Read Aloud > Mark It Up > Discuss**

Look for

Anger

[21] "You have heard that it was said to those of old, 'You shall not murder; and whoever murders will be liable to judgment.' [22] But I say to you that everyone who is angry with his brother will be liable to judgment; whoever insults his brother will be liable to the council; and whoever says, 'You fool!' will be liable to the hell of fire. [23] So if you are offering your gift at the altar and there remember that your brother has something against you, [24] leave your gift there before the altar and go. First be reconciled to your brother, and then come and offer your gift. [25] Come to terms quickly with your accuser while you are going with him to court, lest your accuser hand you over to the judge, and the judge to the guard, and you be put in prison. [26] Truly, I say to you, you will never get out until you have paid the last penny....

Retaliation

MATTHEW 5[38] "You have heard that it was said, 'An eye for an eye and a tooth for a tooth.' [39] But I say to you, Do not resist the one who is evil. But if anyone slaps you on the right cheek, turn to him the other also. [40] And if anyone would sue you and take your tunic, let him have your cloak as well. [41] And if anyone forces you to go one mile, go with him two miles. [42] Give to the one who begs from you, and do not refuse the one who would borrow from you.

Love Your Enemies

[43] "You have heard that it was said, 'You shall love your neighbor and hate your enemy.' [44] But I say to you, Love your enemies and pray for

those who persecute you, [45] so that you may be sons of your Father who is in heaven. For he makes his sun rise on the evil and on the good, and sends rain on the just and on the unjust. [46] For if you love those who love you, what reward do you have? Do not even the tax collectors do the same? [47] And if you greet only your brothers, what more are you doing than others? Do not even the Gentiles do the same? [48] You therefore must be perfect, as your heavenly Father is perfect....

--. ?

--. ?

--. ?

WATCH View Episode 2 (28 min., from 0:00 to 28:23) > **Discuss**

INTRO: Jesus sends out the Twelve on a scary mission to heal others and proclaim the kingdom of God. They are sent out in odd pairings. But he knows what he's doing, even sending **Thomas** to

the SW where he can ask Ramah's dad **Kafni** for her hand in marriage.

--. *What stood out to you about the assignments and pairings made by Jesus?*

... about their response to this mission?

--. *How does he teach them in a playful and purposeful way?*

DISCOVER | Read Aloud > Mark It Up > Discuss

INTRO: The gospels are silent about where Jesus sent out the disciples. The Chosen identifies locations in every direction (see map on page ??)

SOUTH: Matthew and Zee to Jericho

NORTH: Simon and Judas to Caesarea Philippi

WEST: Big James and Little James to the Plains of Sharon

EAST: Andrew and Philip to Naveh

SOUTHWEST: John and Thomas to Joppa

SOUTHEAST: Nathanael and Thaddeus to Peresa

NOTE (in The Chosen) where the disciples were sent

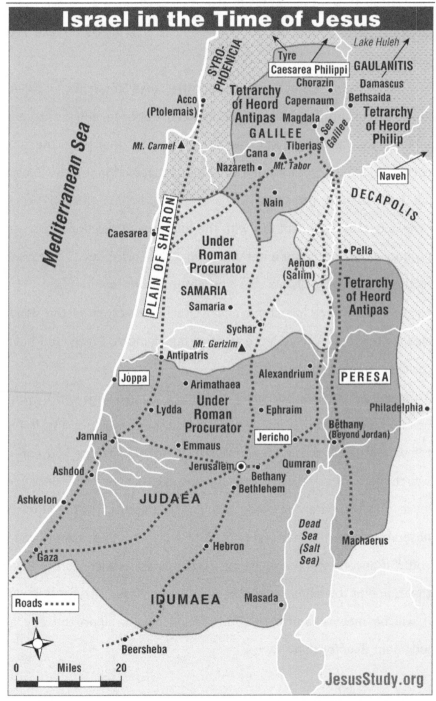

Israel in the Time of Jesus

Lake Huleh

SYRO-PHOENICIA

Tyre

Caesarea Philippi

GAULANITIS

Chorazin

Damascus

Acco (Ptolemais)

Tetrarchy of Heord Antipas

Capernaum

Bethsaida

Magdala

Tetrarchy of Heord Philip

Mt. Carmel ▲

GALILEE

Sea of Galilee

Cana

Tiberias

Nazareth ▲ Mt. Tabor

Naveh

Nain

DECAPOLIS

Mediterranean Sea

Caesarea

PLAIN OF SHARON

Under Roman Procurator

Aenon (Salim)

Pella

SAMARIA

Tetrarchy of Heord Antipas

Samaria

Sychar

Mt. Gerizim ▲

Antipatris

Joppa

Arimathaea

Alexandrium

PERESA

Under Roman Procurator

Ephraim

Philadelphia

Lydda

Jamnia

Emmaus

Jericho

Bethany (Beyond Jordan)

Ashdod

Jerusalem ◉

Qumran

Ashkelon

Bethany

Bethlehem

JUDAEA

Dead Sea (Salt Sea)

Machaerus

Gaza

Hebron

IDUMAEA

Masada

Roads ······

N

0   Miles   20

Beersheba

JesusStudy.org

Jesus Sends Out the Twelve
MATTHEW 10 Jesus called his twelve disciples to him and gave them authority to drive out impure spirits and to heal every disease and sickness.

[2] These are the names of the twelve apostles: first, Simon (who is called Peter) and his brother Andrew; James son of Zebedee, and his brother John; [3] Philip and Bartholomew; Thomas and Matthew the tax collector; James son of Alphaeus, and Thaddaeus; [4] Simon the Zealot and Judas Iscariot, who betrayed him.

[5] These twelve Jesus sent out with the following instructions: "Do not go among the Gentiles or enter any town of the Samaritans. [6] Go rather to the lost sheep of Israel. [7] As you go, proclaim this message: 'The kingdom of heaven has come near.' [8] Heal the sick, raise the dead, cleanse those who have leprosy, drive out demons. Freely you have received; freely give.

[9] "Do not get any gold or silver or copper to take with you in your belts— [10] no bag for the journey or extra shirt or sandals or a staff, for the worker is worth his keep. [11] Whatever town or village you enter, search there for some worthy person and stay at their house until you leave. [12] As you enter the home, give it your greeting. [13] If the home is deserving, let your peace rest on it; if it is not, let your peace return to you. [14] If anyone will not welcome you or listen to your words, leave that home or town and shake the dust off your feet. [15] Truly I tell you, it will be more bearable for Sodom and Gomorrah on the day of judgment than for that town.

--. ?

--. ?

--. ?

RELATE How It Applies to God / Life / You > Discuss

--. ?

--. ?

**After watching > discovering > relating,
What slogan would you write or draw on your T-shirt?**

Draft concepts:

Final design:

NOTES on Study #2 Commentary and Historical Context

MATTHEW 10:1-15—Jesus Sends Out the Twelve

•

•

PASSAGE—Title

•

•

•

PASSAGE—Title

•

•

•

That's plausible but did it happen?

Did Roman bureaucrats dance around the use of force on Jews? Why not just impose Marshall law?

The Romans were concerned to not stir up an insurrection, for which Jesus would later be accused. The differences in approach—as played out by Quintus, Atticus, and Gaius (a secret believer?) —give plausible context to what will happen next.

Did people really drink olive oil, as shown here?

Mediterranean people still believe olive oil has medicinal benefits, whether used in cooking or drinking. More of this tradition is shown in Episode 4.

Given arranged marriages only, could Thomas & Ramah marry for love?

Marriages in Bible times were not made for love, per se, but for the mutual benefit of both families involved. Arranged by the fathers of bride & groom, Jewish marriages would begin with a betrothal/ engagement. A bride price and the groom's gift (not always monetary) are exchanged to seal the deal.

When Jesus sends out the Twelve, were specific assignments given out?

Not in Scripture, but in the film: Simon Peter & Judas to Caesarea Philippi, Andrew & Phillip to Naveh, Nathanael & Thad to Perea, John & Thomas to Joppa, Little & Big James to the Plains of Sharon, Matthew the tax collector & Simon the Zealot to Jericho. See map (pages 137-138).

Drive it HOME Review & Respond: Worship, Journaling, Prayer

?.?

?.?

?.?

Video Insights: What is the Gospel? -Melissa Dougherty
Type in URL: tinyurl.com/the-gospel-defined (20:24 min.)
Notes:

_____

Video Insights: What is the Gospel? -Melissa Dougherty
Type in URL: tinyurl.com/the-gospel-defined (20:24 min.)
Notes:

_____

PRIOR to STUDY

Some reminders

Remember, always tell your group at which question to end, so they know how far to go during the study/discussion time.

Keep up the pace! You often think you have more time than you do, so, closely monitor your time, leave things unsaid, and keep moving to end on time.

NOTE FOR EVERYONE: *Inviting new people—is it too late?* No way! The beauty of *The Chosen Study* is that new members can come in at any time and binge watch to catch up! Additionally, we've seen people go through each Season multiple times.

Who to invite? Anyone who fits on this list: friends, loved ones, family members, colleagues, teammates, acquaintances, those who cross your path—if they're curious, if they're willing to check it—then come!

Two by Two (Ep. 2) &
Physician Heal Thyself (Ep. 3) Study #4

INTRO: ?

DISCOVER Read Aloud > Mark It Up > Discuss

Look For:

Paul's Thorn in the Flesh

2 CORINTHIANS 12 [7] So to keep me from becoming conceited because of the surpassing greatness of the revelations, a thorn was given me in the flesh, a messenger of Satan to harass me, to keep me from becoming conceited. [8] Three times I pleaded with the Lord about this, that it should leave me. [9] But he said to me, "My grace is sufficient for you, for my power is made perfect in weakness." Therefore I will boast all the more gladly of my weaknesses, so that the power of Christ may rest upon me. [10] For the sake of Christ, then, I am content with weaknesses, insults, hardships, persecutions, and calamities. For when I am weak, then I am strong.

--. ?

--.?

--.?

WATCH **View Season Three, Episode 2** *(6 ½ min. from 53:08 to 59.42)* **> Discuss**

INTRO: The two-by-two mission of healing and preaching prompts **Little James** to ask why he hasn't been healed, bringing up the issue of suffering and seemingly unanswered prayer.

--**1.** *How do you relate to this universal true-to-life mystery of unanswered prayer represented by Little James in the film and in real life?*

--. ?

--. ?

WATCH View Season Three, Episode 3 (50 min. from 00:24 to 50:23) > Discuss

INTRO: Jesus' hometown of Nazareth is the scene of much merriment and a local festival, where he literally drops the ball (often) and is teased for that. He's asked to read and interpret the  Scriptures as a special guest preacher in the local synagogue. His interpretation of Isaiah is authoritative yet at odds with Rabbinic tradition. That's when things turn deadly serious; the hometown boy is driven by angry synagogue rulers to the edge of a cliff outside the city, to be killed.

--2. *What do you make of the fumbling humanity and divine authority of Jesus on full display here?*

–3. *Why and how did Jesus provoke the anger of his hometown audience?*

--4. *Why and how did he manage to escape getting killed this time?*

DISCOVER Read Aloud > Mark It Up > Discuss

NOTE:

(See page 61 for some historical background.)

Look For:

Jesus Begins his Ministry

LUKE 4: [14] And Jesus returned in the power of the Spirit to Galilee, and a report about him went out through all the surrounding country. [15] And he taught in their synagogues, being glorified by all.

[16] And he came to Nazareth, where he had been brought up. As was his custom, he went to the synagogue on the Sabbath day, and he stood up to read. [17] And the scroll of the prophet Isaiah was given to him. He unrolled the scroll and found the place where it was written,

> [18] "The Spirit of the Lord is upon me,
>
> > because he has anointed me
> >
> > to proclaim good news to the poor.
>
> He has sent me to proclaim liberty to the captives
>
> > and recovering of sight to the blind,
> >
> > to set at liberty those who are oppressed,
>
> [19] to proclaim the year of the Lord's favor."

[20] And he rolled up the scroll and gave it back to the attendant and sat down. And the eyes of all in the synagogue were fixed on him. [21] And he began to say to them, "Today this Scripture has been fulfilled in your hearing."

²² And all spoke well of him and marveled at the gracious words that were coming from his mouth. And they said, "Is not this Joseph's son?" ²³ And he said to them, "Doubtless you will quote to me this proverb, '"Physician, heal yourself." What we have heard you did at Capernaum, do here in your hometown as well.'"

²⁴ And he said, "Truly, I say to you, no prophet is acceptable in his hometown. ²⁵ But in truth, I tell you, there were many widows in Israel in the days of Elijah, when the heavens were shut up three years and six months, and a great famine came over all the land, ²⁶ and Elijah was sent to none of them but only to Zarephath, in the land of Sidon, to a woman who was a widow. ²⁷ And there were many lepers in Israel in the time of the prophet Elisha, and none of them was cleansed, but only Naaman the Syrian."

²⁸ When they heard these things, all in the synagogue were filled with wrath. ²⁹ And they rose up and drove him out of the town and brought him to the brow of the hill on which their town was built, so that they could throw him down the cliff. ³⁰ But passing through their midst, he went away.

--. ?

--. ?

RELATE How It Applies to God / Life / You > Discuss

--. ?

--. ?

After watching > discovering > relating, What slogan would you write or draw on your T-shirt?

Draft concept:

Final design:

NOTES on Study #4 — Commentary and Historical Context

PASSAGE—Title

•

•

PASSAGE—Title

•

•

•

PASSAGE—Title

•

•

•

That's plausible but did it happen?

It's hard to imagine Jesus as playful, comedic, or hungry, yet this film does. Doesn't such creative authority add too much to Scripture?

Jesus' hometown Nazareth is the scene of much merriment and festivities, where he literally drops the ball (often) and is teased for that. Such natural mother-child and other hometown interactions add depth and context and enhance Jesus' humanity in ways that text alone cannot. Thus, Jesus' full child-like humanity—clumsy & funny, tired & hungry—is on full display.

Mary and Jesus both say they "miss" Joseph. When did he die?
That's unknown to us. The last biblical allusion to Joseph tending to Jesus is in Luke 2, where the boy Jesus (age 12) is engaged in Q & A in the Temple. Later (see below), Joseph reflects on his relatively short life as a dad to Jesus.

Did Jesus work with wood? or with stone (as his dad predicted)?
The flashback scene depicts Joseph (and Jesus) working with wood, which he admits is "the wrong profession, given how much stone was around." And so, Joseph pushes Jesus to work with stone. The Greek word describing Jesus and his father's occupation is **tekton,** often **(mis)**translated as *carpenter* (Matthew 13:55; Mark 6:3). Jesus probably spoke the Aramaic (and Hebrew) word **haras**, which means builder or craftsman. Accounting for the Jewish cultural context and Israel's rocky landscape, these two words—and Jesus' profession—are more accurately rendered as *stonemason, craftsman,* or *builder.* Knowing this also helps explain why so many of Jesus' metaphorical illustrations involved stones: foundations, cornerstones, towers, temple stones, rocks, walls, winepresses, and millstones. Case in point: "Which of you, if your son asks for bread, will give him a **stone**?" (Matthew 7:9).

Did Lazarus really push Jesus to preach in his hometown synagogue?
It's not known how the connection was made, but guest preachers or "pulpit supply" were a thing, then as now. Whether at Lazarus's instigation or not, Jesus is asked to read and interpret the Scriptures in the local synagogue.

Did Jesus ever say, "I am the Law of Moses!"—a blasphemy that outrages?
Yes, in so many words. All the NT writers stressed or assumed that the OT, rightly understood, points to Christ as the new Moses (Deuteronomy 18:15; Matthew 5:17-20; Mark 9:2-13; Luke 24:25-27,44; John 5:45-47). Jesus' interpretation of Isaiah is thus normative and authoritative, yet at odds with Rabbinic tradition. When things turned deadly serious, the hometown boy is driven by outraged synagogue rulers to be pushed off a cliff outside the city. But, as we know (Luke 4:14-30), Jesus simply walked away, unscathed.

What place does this mule's bridal have in Jesus' life? In Scripture?
This extrabiblical bridal—a family heirloom in this film—foreshadows the day when Jesus would ride a donkey into Jerusalem in triumphal return and to fulfill Zechariah's prophecy (9:9; see Matthew 21:1-9).

Drive it HOME Review & Respond: Worship, Journaling, Prayer

--.?

--.?

--.?

Video Insights: What is the Gospel? -Melissa Dougherty

Type in URL: tinyurl.com/the-gospel-defined (20:24 min.)

Notes:

Video Insights: What is the Gospel? -Melissa Dougherty

Type in URL: tinyurl.com/the-gospel-defined (20:24 min.)

Notes:

Video Insights: What is the Gospel? -Melissa Dougherty

Type in URL: tinyurl.com/the-gospel-defined (20:24 min.)

Notes:

Another reminder

NOTE TO EVERYONE: *HOME REFLECTION.* Maybe you have not yet gotten to this section (as on pages 30-31, 39-41, and 51-53). No problem. Just don't miss this upcoming "at home" *Reflection* section (pages 71-73). The questions will help you deepen your relationship with God.

And, the *Real But Realistic* sections are nothing, if not entertaining!

Clean, Part 1 (Ep. 4)

Study #5

FROM
The BIBLE

INTRO:

--Focus on Scripture being a critical part of a Jesus' followers life.

DISCOVER Read Aloud > Mark It Up > Discuss

Look For:

Josiah Reigns in Judah

2 KINGS 22 Josiah was eight years old when he began to reign, and he reigned thirty-one years in Jerusalem. His mother's name was Jedidah the daughter of Adaiah of Bozkath. [2] And he did what was right in the eyes of the Lord and walked in all the way of David his father, and he did not turn aside to the right or to the left.

Josiah Repairs the Temple

[3] In the eighteenth year of King Josiah, the king sent, the secretary, to the house of the Lord [to oversee repairs].

Hilkiah Finds the Book of the Law

[8] And Hilkiah the high priest said to Shaphan the secretary, "I have found the Book of the Law in the house of the Lord." . . .

[11] When the king heard the words of the Book of the Law, he tore his clothes. [12] And the king commanded Hilkiah the priest. . .saying, [13] "Go, inquire of the Lord for me, and for the people, and for all Judah, concerning the words of this book that has been found. For great is the wrath of the Lord that is kindled against us, because our fathers have not obeyed the words of this book, to do according to all that is written concerning us." . . . And they [those Josiah sent] brought back word to the king [confirming that God will honor a "penitent, humble heart"].

Josiah's Reforms

23 Then the king sent, and all the elders of Judah and Jerusalem were gathered to him. [2] And the king went up to the house of the Lord, and with him all the men of Judah and all the inhabitants of Jerusalem and the priests and the prophets, all the people, both small and great. And he read in their hearing all the words of the Book of the Covenant that had been found in the house of the Lord. ³ And the king stood by the pillar and made a covenant before the Lord, to walk after the Lord and to keep his commandments and his testimonies and his statutes with all his heart and all his soul, to perform the words of this covenant that were written in this book. And all the people joined in the covenant. [**WHAT FOLLOWS** is a partial list of what King Josiah did]:

—⁴ And the king commanded Hilkiah the high priest and the priests of the second order and the keepers of the threshold to bring out of the temple of the Lord all the vessels made for Baal, for Asherah, and for all the host of heaven. He burned them outside Jerusalem in the fields of the Kidron and carried their ashes to Bethel.

—⁵ And he deposed the priests whom the kings of Judah had ordained to make offerings in the high places at the cities of Judah and around Jerusalem; those also who burned incense to Baal, to the sun and the moon and the constellations and all the host of the heavens.

—⁶ And he brought out the Asherah from the house of the Lord, outside Jerusalem, to the brook Kidron, and burned it at the brook Kidron and beat it to dust and cast the dust of it upon the graves of the common people.

—⁷ And he broke down the houses of the male cult prostitutes who were in the house of the Lord, where the women wove hangings for the Asherah.

—[8] And he brought all the priests out of the cities of Judah, and defiled the high places where the priests had made offerings, from Geba to Beersheba.

—And he broke down the high places of the gates that were at the entrance of the gate of Joshua the governor of the city, which were on one's left at the gate of the city. . . .

—[10] And he defiled Topheth, which is in the Valley of the Son of Hinnom, that no one might burn his son or his daughter as an offering to Molech.

—[11] And he removed the horses that the kings of Judah had dedicated to the sun, at the entrance to the house of the Lord, by the chamber of Nathanmelech the chamberlain, which was in the precincts.

—And he burned the chariots of the sun with fire.

—[12] And the altars on the roof of the upper chamber of Ahaz, which the kings of Judah had made, and the altars that Manasseh had made in the two courts of the house of the Lord, he pulled down and broke in pieces and cast the dust of them into the brook Kidron.

—[13] And the king defiled the high places that were east of Jerusalem, to the south of the mount of corruption, which Solomon the king of Israel had built for Ashtoreth the abomination of the Sidonians, and for Chemosh the abomination of Moab, and for Milcom the abomination of the Ammonites.

—[14] And he broke in pieces the pillars and cut down the Asherim and filled their places with the bones of men.

—¹⁵ Moreover, the altar at Bethel, the high place erected by Jeroboam the son of Nebat, who made Israel to sin, that altar with the high place he pulled down and burned, reducing it to dust. He also burned the Asherah. . . .

—¹⁹ And Josiah removed all the shrines also of the high places that were in the cities of Samaria, which kings of Israel had made, provoking the Lord to anger. He did to them according to all that he had done at Bethel. ²⁰ And he sacrificed all the priests of the high places who were there, on the altars, and burned human bones on them. Then he returned to Jerusalem.

--, ?

--, ?

--, ?

WATCH **View Episode 4** *(47 min., from 0:00 to 46:43)* **> Discuss**

INTRO: The cast of main characters returns to Capernaum. We get a "taste and see" (black & white clips, no sound) of the 2x2 mission that the disciples were sent out on. We also get a glimpse into the marital dynamics of **Peter and Eden.** Their spat will feel very familiar to all couples. We are introduced to synagogue ruler **Jairus** and **his 12-y-o daughter** who takes ill from unclean city water, as well as to a woman with a continuous issue of blood (named **Veronica** in this film), setting us up for two future healings, no doubt.

--. How does the film depict the two-by-two mission of the apostles?

--. Where do you see yourself in the marital dynamics of Peter and Eden?

--. ?

DISCOVER | **Read Aloud > Mark It Up > Discuss**

INTRO:

Look for:

Paul and Silas in Thessalonica

ACTS 17 Now when they had passed through Amphipolis and Apollonia, they came to Thessalonica, where there was a synagogue of the Jews. [2] And Paul went in, as was his custom, and on three Sabbath days he reasoned with them from the Scriptures, [3] explaining and proving that it was necessary for the Christ to suffer and to rise from the dead, and saying, "This Jesus, whom I proclaim to you, is the Christ." [4] And some of them were persuaded and joined Paul and Silas, as did a great many of the devout Greeks and not a few of the leading women. [5] But the Jews were jealous, and taking some wicked men of the rabble, they formed a mob, set the city in an uproar, and attacked the house of Jason, seeking to bring them out to the crowd. [6] And when they could not find them, they dragged Jason and some of the brothers before the city authorities, shouting, "These men who have turned the world upside down have come here also, [7] and Jason has received them, and they are all acting against the decrees of Caesar, saying that there is another king, Jesus." [8] And the people and the city authorities were disturbed when they heard these things. [9] And when they had taken money as security from Jason and the rest, they let them go.

Paul and Silas in Berea

[10] The brothers immediately sent Paul and Silas away by night to Berea, and when they arrived they went into the Jewish synagogue. [11] Now these Jews were more noble than those in Thessalonica; they received the word with all eagerness, examining the Scriptures daily to see if these things were so. [12] Many of them therefore believed, with not a few Greek women of high standing as well as men.

--. ?

--. ?

--. ?

| RELATE | How It Applies to God / Life / You > Discuss

--. ?

--. ?

After watching > discovering > relating,
What slogan would you write or draw on your T-shirt?

Draft concepts:

Final design:

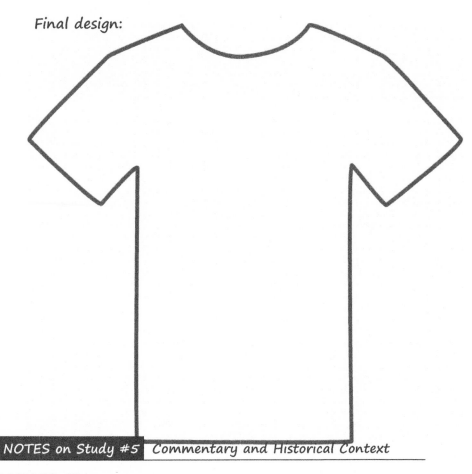

NOTES on Study #5 Commentary and Historical Context

PASSAGE—Title

-

-

PASSAGE—Title

-

-

-

PASSAGE—Title

-

-

-

REALISTIC
But REAL?

That's plausible but did it happen?

Do we really know what the two-by-two mission accomplished?
No more than the disciples themselves seemed to know. The Twelve reunite in Capernaum to debrief and gain some understanding of the powerful impact God made through them. They, like us, were in awe.

Is Jesus mentioned in the Torah—or not!?
Not by name. But in their reading of Torah, Rabbi Jussif and synagogue ruler Jairus anticipate a military, even messianic, figure—one like Jesus. Christians see Jesus in "types" (foreshadowing a messianic figure) implicit in the first five books. For example, he is "the offspring of the woman would eventually crush the serpent's head" (Genesis 3:15; Romans 16:20). Christians believe Jesus is "the prophet greater than Moses" who would come (Deuteronomy 15:18). Even Jewish Talmudic scholars have thought the prophecy that "the scepter shall not depart from Judah until Shiloh comes" (Genesis 49:10) is Messianic. But Jewish leaders, both in this film and in real life, implicate Jesus as a dangerous false prophet. So, was the Messiah foretold in Torah? No doubt. Is Jesus that Messiah? As the debate roils on, you get to decide.

What are we to make of the broken cistern?
It becomes a Jewish problem, instead of Rome's. Fixing it together allows Peter and Gaius to bond. Later, Jairus' 12-y-o daughter Nili takes ill from unclean city water. So, broken cisterns have become a public health crisis.

What are we to make of the Tamar-and-Mary Magdalene tension?
The tension (and teamwork!) between these two has been evident since Episode 1 and will continue in Episode 6. Just now, these two women join other female entrepreneurs—a woman with a continuous issue of blood (named Veronica in this film) and Eden (wife of Simon Peter). Each exchange of grievances and resources sets the stage for future reconciliation.

What are we to make of the marital dynamics of Peter & Eden?
As much as you want to. Their ongoing spat feels very familiar to all couples.

Drive it HOME | Review & Respond: Worship, Journaling, Prayer

--. ?

--. ?

--. ?

Video Insights: What is the Gospel? -Melissa Dougherty

Type in URL: tinyurl.com/the-gospel-defined (20:24 min.)

Notes:

_____

Video Insights: What is the Gospel? *-Melissa Dougherty*

Type in URL: tinyurl.com/the-gospel-defined (20:24 min.)

Notes:

_____

Video Insights: What is the Gospel? *-Melissa Dougherty*

Type in URL: tinyurl.com/the-gospel-defined (20:24 min.)

Notes:

_____

 **Getting ready now for your last gathering.**

Please read the "Prior" note on page 118 (and its reference on page 15) regarding a longer event or retreat for Study #10.

If you haven't already done so, work on plans for your last gathering, to get it on your group members' schedules, if different than your normal meeting time.

Clean, Part 2 (Ep. 5)

Study #6

INTRO: Fasting and New Wine

FROM *the* BIBLE

DISCOVER Read Aloud > Mark It Up > Discuss

Look For:

Question About Fasting
MARK 2 [18] Now John's disciples and the Pharisees were fasting. And people came and said to him, "Why do John's disciples and the disciples of the Pharisees fast, but your disciples do not fast?"

[19] And Jesus said to them, "Can the wedding guests fast while the bridegroom is with them? As long as they have the bridegroom with them, they cannot fast. [20] The days will come when the bridegroom is taken away from them, and then they will fast in that day.

[21] No one sews a piece of unshrunk cloth on an old garment. If he does, the patch tears away from it, the new from the old, and a worse tear is made. [22] And no one puts new wine into old wineskins. If he does, the wine will burst the skins—and the wine is destroyed, and so are the skins. But new wine is for fresh wineskins."

--. ?

--. ?

--. ?

WATCH **View Episode 5** (53 min., from 1:48 –54:24) **> Discuss**

INTRO: Synagogue ruler **Jairus** intends to get his 12-y-o daughter **Nili** healed, which means getting Jesus there in time. But Jesus' entourage is interrupted by **Veronica**, whose continuous issue of blood (going on 12 years) is cause for shaming her as "unclean" and excluding her from Jesus. Jesus must deal with competing demands, delays, and expectations. How he pulls this off makes for an inspiring and redemptive episode.

--1. *What do you suppose was going on in the mind of Jairus before Jesus arrived?*

*... of **his wife Michal**?*

*... of **his 12-year-old daughter Nili***?

--2. *What's going on in the mind of Veronica before touching Jesus?*

... of Jesus as he is being touched by her?

... of the onlookers, pro-and-con, as they see what happened between the two?

--. ?

DISCOVER *Read Aloud > Mark It Up > Discuss*

INTRO: Faith does not cure cancer. It cures sin. And sin is a much more dire problem than the most life-threatening of diseases.

FROM The BIBLE

During the poor woman's ordeal, her incurable disease had drained her, not only of her energy, but also of all her money. Her quest to find a cure from the physicians had solved nothing; in fact, she had gotten worse under their care....

Look For:

Jesus Heals a Woman and Jairus' Daughter

MARK 2: [21] And when Jesus had crossed again in the boat to the other side, a great crowd gathered about him, and he was beside the sea. [22] Then came one of the rulers of the synagogue, Jairus by name, and seeing him, he fell at his feet [23] and implored him earnestly, saying, "My little daughter is at the point of death. Come and lay your hands on her, so that she may be made well and live." [24] And he went with him.

And a great crowd followed him and thronged about him. [25] And there was a woman who had had a discharge of blood for twelve years, [26] and who had suffered much under many physicians, and had spent all that she had, and was no better but rather grew worse. [27] She had heard the reports about Jesus and came up behind him in the crowd and touched his garment. [28] For she said, "If I touch even his garments, I will be made well." [29] And immediately the flow of blood dried up, and she felt in her body that she was healed of her disease. [30] And Jesus, perceiving in himself that power had gone out from him, immediately turned about in the crowd and said, "Who touched my garments?" **31** And his disciples said to him, "You see the crowd pressing around you, and yet you say, 'Who touched me?'" **32** And he looked around to see who had done it. **33** But the woman, knowing what had happened to her, came in fear and trembling and fell down before him and told him the whole truth. **34** And he said to her, "Daughter, your faith has made you well; go in peace, and be healed of your disease."

35 While he was still speaking, there came from the ruler's house some who said, "Your daughter is dead. Why trouble the Teacher any further?"

36 But overhearing what they said, Jesus said to the ruler of the synagogue, "Do not fear, only believe." **37** And he allowed no one to follow him except Peter and James and John the brother of James. **38** They came to the house of the ruler of the synagogue, and Jesus saw a commotion, people weeping and wailing loudly. **39** And when he had entered, he said to them, "Why are you making a commotion and weeping? The child is not dead but sleeping."

40 And they laughed at him. But he put them all outside and took the child's father and mother and those who were with him and went in where the child was. **41** Taking her by the hand he said to her, "Talitha cumi," which means, "Little girl, I say to you, arise." **42** And immediately the girl got up and began walking (for she was twelve years of age), and they were immediately overcome with amazement. **43** And he strictly charged them that no one should know this, and told them to give her something to eat.

--. ?

--. ?

RELATE How It Applies to God / Life / You > Discuss

--. ?

--. ?

After watching > discovering > relating,

What slogan would you write or draw on your T-shirt?

Draft concepts:

Final design:

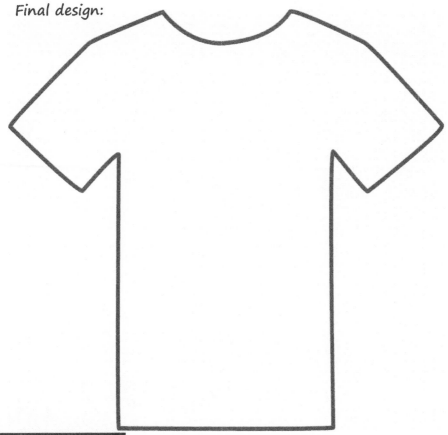

PASSAGE—Title

•

•

PASSAGE—Title

•

•

•

PASSAGE—Title

•

•

•

REALISTIC But REAL?   *That's plausible but did it happen?*

Was the daughter of Jarius "with child"? and sickened by the bad water?
The film ties the two events together. Pure speculation but, in either event, she is sick unto death. Synagogue ruler Jairus intends to get his 12-y-o daughter healed by Jesus, but never imagines the Messiah he's been reading about, and has seen do miracles, will now also raise the dead.

Did Simon Peter and Quintus work hand in hand to fix the water system?
Such a public health crisis in ancient Israel is likely. Their collaboration, however unlikely, provides context for what happens next in Jew-Roman relations and in Jairus's child (dying of filthy water) eventually getting well.

The woman issuing blood for 12 years finally got to meet Jesus after all. Was that "God-appointment" pre-arranged? or spur-of-the-moment?
Jesus' entourage is interrupted by this woman, as recorded in Luke 8:41-56. Named Veronica in the film, she is determined to get through—and does with the help of the two disciples who first met by the water's edge. This encounter, by chance or pre-determined, outraged Pharisees who tried to block her. Hers is a *cause célèbre*, due to community standards shaming her as "unclean" and excluding her from Jesus. Jesus deals with these competing demands, delays, and expectations in ways that inspire all to come forward.

Did Jesus really expect everyone to keep secret the miracle at Jairus' home? If so, why?
Gospel accounts vary on this. Yes, per Mark & Luke but not Matthew. What Jesus asked for—to not tell anyone what they had witnessed—proved to be a poorly kept secret. No doubt, word leaked from Simon, James, John, Jairus, Michal (the mom), or Nili (the daughter). Still, the so-called "Messianic Secret" derives from this private incident and similar ones (Matthew 8:4; 9:30; 16:20; Mark 3:12; Luke 9:21). In urging secrecy, Jesus was not using reverse psychology but sensed that too much publicity to his healing miracles would hinder his teaching

ministry, and he did not want his death to come prematurely and thus jeopardize his ultimate mission.

Drive it HOME | Review & Respond: Worship, Journaling, Prayer

--. ?

--. ?

--. ?

Video Insights: What is the Gospel? -Melissa Dougherty
Type in URL: tinyurl.com/the-gospel-defined (20:24 min.)

Notes:

Video Insights: What is the Gospel? -Melissa Dougherty
Type in URL: tinyurl.com/the-gospel-defined (20:24 min.)
Notes:

Video Insights: What is the Gospel? -Melissa Dougherty
Type in URL: tinyurl.com/the-gospel-defined (20:24 min.)
Notes:

Getting ready for Study #7

NOTE FOR EVERYONE:

Intensity in Tent City (Ep. 6) Study #7

INTRO: ?? FROM THE BIBLE

FROM
The CHOSEN

WATCH **View Episode 6** *(50 min., from 0:00 to 49:48)* **> Discuss**

INTRO:
Pilate hears about Jesus—from his wife (who dreamt of Jesus) and his colleague **Atticus** (who spies on Jesus). The disciples prepare for worst-case scenarios and try to quell the crisis their preaching in Decapolis has created. **Gaius'** loyalty is questioned by his Roman superior (Dominus), as Gaius shows sympathy to Jesus' followers. **Tamar** and **Mary Magdalene** disagree on how to show loyalty to Jesus with all that they are and have. **Andrew & Philip** handle a crisis involving **John the Baptist,** languishing in prison but expressing doubts about Jesus. **Simon the Zealot's** pursuers finally corner him and question his loyalty to Jesus and to their cause.

1. *What foreshadowing of future plot twists do you see in this episode?*

2. *What are you hoping will happen in the film, that you are not quite sure about from Scripture?*

--. ?

DISCOVER **Read Aloud > Study > Discuss**

INTRO: Leprosy is a debilitating and disfiguring nerve disease. It can now be cured, but in pre-scientific Israel, it was misunderstood and feared. In fact, the rabbis said it was easier to raise the dead than to cure leprosy. This leper, like the

FROM The BIBLE

paralytic described next, had no hope of a cure, and was rejected by society (Leviticus 13:46).

Look for:

Messengers from John the Baptist

MATTHEW 11 When Jesus had finished instructing his twelve disciples, he went on from there to teach and preach in their cities.

[2] Now when John heard in prison about the deeds of the Christ, he sent word by his disciples [3] and said to him, "Are you the one who is to come, or shall we look for another?" [4] And Jesus answered them, "Go and tell John what you hear and see: [5] the blind receive their sight and the lame walk, lepers are cleansed and the deaf hear, and the dead are raised up, and the poor have good news preached to them. [6] And blessed is the one who is not offended by me."

[7] As they went away, Jesus began to speak to the crowds concerning John: "What did you go out into the wilderness to see? A reed shaken by the wind? [8] What then did you go out to see? A man dressed in soft clothing? Behold, those who wear soft clothing are in kings' houses. [9] What then did you go out to see? A prophet? Yes, I tell you, and more than a prophet. [10] This is he of whom it is written,

"'Behold, I send my messenger before your face,

who will prepare your way before you.'

[11] Truly, I say to you, among those born of women there has arisen no one greater than John the Baptist. Yet the one who is least in the kingdom of heaven is greater than he. [12] From the days of John the Baptist until now the kingdom of heaven has suffered violence, and the violent take it by force. [13] For all the Prophets and the Law prophesied until John, [14] and if you are willing to accept it, he is Elijah who is to come. [15] He who has ears to hear, let him hear.

16 "But to what shall I compare this generation? It is like children sitting in the marketplaces and calling to their playmates,

17 "'We played the flute for you, and you did not dance;

we sang a dirge, and you did not mourn.'

18 For John came neither eating nor drinking, and they say, 'He has a demon.' 19 The Son of Man came eating and drinking, and they say, 'Look at him! A glutton and a drunkard, a friend of tax collectors and sinners!' Yet wisdom is justified by her deeds."

--. ?

--. ?

--. ?

RELATE How It Applies to God / Life / You > Discuss

--. ?

--. ?

After watching > discovering > relating,
What slogan would you write or draw on your T-shirt?

Draft concepts:

Final design:

NOTES on Study #7 Commentary and Historical Context

Passage—Title

- ?

- ?

Passage—Title

- ?

- ?

Passage—Title

- ?

- ?

REALISTIC But REAL?

That's plausible but did it happen?

Did Pilate's wife dream of Jesus and the serpent in the Garden?

Possibly. Her dream of Jesus as "innocent" causes her "great suffering" (Matthew 27:19), denoted by a real slithering snake (symbolic of Satan).

Did the disciples' preaching in Decapolis create such a fearful crisis?

Their message caused healing *and* controversy (Matthew 10:5-17; Mark 6:7-12; Luke 9:1-6). The disciples, no doubt, huddled in fear of the dire consequences Jesus predicted. That Gentile groups of the Decapolis, named in the film, turn against the disciples—that is conjecture. Jesus forbade visiting Gentiles (Matthew 10:5), but the Twelve may have done so, anyway. Or word spread wildly beyond their assignment to reach only fellow Jews.

Did Tamar & Mary Magdalene fight over status, loyalty & business?

The two entrepreneurs disagree as realistically as men do. They are among many women who traveled with Jesus to support his ministry (Luke 8:2-3). That Tamar would sell her beautiful heirloom necklace is an example of giving "out of their own means." Women did not own land or property back then, so their wealth was conveyed via fine jewelry. Their engagement in a vineyard business of James's and John's father is pure speculation.

Did Pilate debate the use of force with his Roman colleagues, e.g., Atticus?

Conjecture, meant to typify the wishy-washy, people-pleasing Pilate, who'd later be swayed by crowds to crucify Jesus. That the fictional Atticus went undercover, as an informant to Rome, also fills gaps in the biblical account.

Why so much commotion around Peter's house?

That Peter's home was the center of activity and conflict is natural, as he was the only disciple known to have a wife. Pity Simon and Eden as they try to make up for lost time and a lost baby. Archaeologists found (in 1968) the ruins of a large house in ancient Capernaum believed to be Peter's home.

How did John & Big James, with Peter & Jesus, placate John the Baptist?

Someone had to. Jesus' strongest believer, John the Baptist, is languishing in prison and expressing doubts but was reassured by Jesus (Matthew 11:2-29; Luke 7:18-35). Jesus' on-the-spot miraculous healings placate John the Baptist's messengers but infuriate the authorities—in accord with Scripture.

Did Simon the Zealot's pursuers finally corner him and question his loyalty to their cause?

Again, this extrabiblical cinematic flair fills in the gaps and shows how Jesus changes the loyalties of those he calls. Likewise, Gaius' loyalty is questioned by his Roman handler (Dominus), for showing mercy to Jesus' followers.

Drive it HOME Review & Respond: Worship, Journaling, Prayer

--. ?

--. ?

--. ?

Video Insights: What is the Gospel? -Melissa Dougherty
Type in URL: tinyurl.com/the-gospel-defined (20:24 min.)
Notes:

_____

Video Insights: What is the Gospel? -Melissa Dougherty
Type in URL: tinyurl.com/the-gospel-defined (20:24 min.)
Notes:

_____

Video Insights: What is the Gospel? -Melissa Dougherty
Type in URL: tinyurl.com/the-gospel-defined (20:24 min.)
Notes:

_____

 **Getting ready for your last gathering.**

Okay, we won't bother you anymore after this, but please read the "Prior" note on page 118 (and its reference on page 15 regarding a longer event or retreat as an alternative for Study #10.

If you haven't already done so, finalize your plans for your last gathering to get it on your group members' schedules, if it is different than your normal meeting time.

Ears To Hear (Episode 7)

Study #8

INTRO: Big storylines ("Get used to different"), parables, and Jewish culture (feast of Purim, prayer tassels) set up the Grand Finale!

https://www.jesusfilm.org/blog/parable-great-banquet/

WATCH **View Episode 7** (11 min., from 0:00-12:04) **> Discuss ??????**

INTRO: Scene opens with **Jairus** celebrating the Feast of Purim, then onto **Matthew & Mary Magdalene** until **Thomas** interrupts, returning without Ramah, who evidently stays behind to "work on" her dad.

--**1.** *What larger storylines are advanced in this opening scene?*

--**2.** *What do you learn about Jewish culture in this episode?*

--**3.** *Who's listening to whom, in a most helpful way?*

... And who's NOT listening and, thus, only exacerbating the situation?

DISCOVER **Read Aloud > Mark It Up > Discuss**

INTRO: What

Look for....
Healing of a Man on the Sabbath

LUKE 14 One Sabbath, when he went to dine at the house of a ruler of the Pharisees, they were watching him carefully. ² And behold, there was a man before him who had dropsy. ³ And Jesus responded to the lawyers and Pharisees, saying, "Is it lawful to heal on the Sabbath, or not?" ⁴ But they remained silent. Then he took him and healed him and sent him away. ⁵ And he said to them, "Which of you, having a son or an ox that has fallen into a well on a Sabbath day, will not immediately pull him out?" ⁶ And they could not reply to these things.

The Parable of the Wedding Feast

⁷ Now he told a parable to those who were invited, when he noticed how they chose the places of honor, saying to them, ⁸ "When you are invited by someone to a wedding feast, do not sit down in a place of honor, lest someone more distinguished than you be invited by him, ⁹ and he who invited you both will come and say to you, 'Give your place to this person,' and then you will begin with shame to take the lowest place. ¹⁰ But when you are invited, go and sit in the lowest place, so that when your host comes he may say to you, 'Friend, move up higher.' Then you will be honored in the presence of all who sit at table with you. ¹¹ For everyone who exalts himself will be humbled, and he who humbles himself will be exalted."

The Parable of the Great Banquet

¹² He said also to the man who had invited him, "When you give a dinner or a banquet, do not invite your friends or your brothers or your relatives or rich neighbors, lest they also invite you in return and you be repaid. ¹³ But when you give a feast, invite the poor, the crippled,

the lame, the blind, [14] and you will be blessed, because they cannot repay you. For you will be repaid at the resurrection of the just."

[15] When one of those who reclined at table with him heard these things, he said to him, "Blessed is everyone who will eat bread in the kingdom of God!"

[16] But he said to him, "A man once gave a great banquet and invited many. [17] And at the time for the banquet he sent his servant to say to those who had been invited, 'Come, for everything is now ready.' [18] But they all alike began to make excuses. The first said to him, 'I have bought a field, and I must go out and see it. Please have me excused.' [19] And another said, 'I have bought five yoke of oxen, and I go to examine them. Please have me excused.' [20] And another said, 'I have married a wife, and therefore I cannot come.' [21] So the servant came and reported these things to his master. Then the master of the house became angry and said to his servant, 'Go out quickly to the streets and lanes of the city, and bring in the poor and crippled and blind and lame.' [22] And the servant said, 'Sir, what you commanded has been done, and still there is room.' [23] And the master said to the servant, 'Go out to the highways and hedges and compel people to come in, that my house may be filled. [24] For I tell you, none of those men who were invited shall taste my banquet.'"

--. ?

--. ?

??????????

WATCH **View Episode 7** *(26 min., from 11:04-36:46)* **> Discuss**

INTRO: Andrew & Philip are still anxious about a crisis they may have provoked among Gentiles in the Decapolis. **Rabbi Shmuel** hopes to catch Jesus in heresy. **Simon** roams the Roman quarter, as if lost, and is protected by **Gaius**, who brings him home. There Peter sees that **Gaius's** slave/son is sick, raising interest in "the Jewish doctor." **Matthew** denies the Jewish roots of his faith but finally agrees to receive an old man's gift of ancient prayer tassels to settle a tax liability. **Mary** sees this gesture as a "dove" or sign from God speaking to Matthew's sense of unworthiness.

Look for plot twists that you want to see resolved in this film.

--1. *Is a "thing" developing between Simon and Gaius? Explain what you think is going on here.*

--2. *Is a "thing" developing between Matthew & Mary Magdalene? Explain what you think is going on here.*

DISCOVER **Read Aloud > Mark It Up > Discuss**

INTRO: What

Look for....

The Parable of the Dishonest Manager

16 He also said to the disciples, "There was a rich man who had a manager, and charges were brought to him that this man was wasting his possessions. **2** And he called him and said to him, 'What is this that I hear about you? Turn in the account of your management, for you can no longer be manager.' **3** And the manager said to himself, 'What shall I do, since my master is taking the management away from me? I am not strong enough to dig, and I am ashamed to beg. **4** I have decided what to do, so that when I am removed from management, people may receive me into their houses.' **5** So, summoning his master's debtors one by one, he said to the first, 'How much do you owe my master?' **6** He said, 'A hundred measures of oil.' He said to him, 'Take your bill, and sit down quickly and write fifty.' **7** Then he said to another, 'And how much do you owe?' He said, 'A hundred measures of wheat.' He said to him, 'Take your bill, and write eighty.' **8** The master commended the dishonest manager for his shrewdness. For the sons of this world are more shrewd in dealing with their own generation than the sons of light. **9** And I tell you, make friends for yourselves by means of unrighteous wealth, so that when it fails they may receive you into the eternal dwellings.

--, ?

--, ?

WATCH **View Ep. 7** *(25 min., from 36:46-101:50)* **> Discuss**

INTRO: An embarrassed **Matthew** attaches prayer tassels to his robe. **Simon Peter** and **Gaius** visit about embarrassing marital issues, this time concerning Gaius and his wife **Lydia**. Jesus tells  **John** to stay behind to coax and bring a sad recalcitrant Simon along. **Andrew & Philip** are in over their heads with a crisis that provokes Gentiles to riot, typified by **Nashan** and **Fatiyah**. **Jesus** urges one and all to listen and move on, setting up a grand Finale.

--1. *What do the prayer tassels mean to the old man?*

... to Matthew?

... to Mary?

--2. *How is Jesus able to both stir and calm the waters that divide the fractious groups at the Decapolis?*

RELATE *How It Applies to God / Life / You* **> Discuss**

--. ?

--. ?

After watching > discovering > relating,
What slogan would you write or draw on your T-shirt?

Draft concepts:

Final design:

NOTES on Study #8 Commentary and Historical Context

Passage—Title

• ?

• ?

Passage—Title

• ?

• ?

Passage—Title

• ?

• ?

That's plausible but did it happen?

What is it that stirred up trouble at the "highways & hedges"?

This expression stems from Jesus' Parable of the Banquet (Matthew 22:1-14; Luke 14:15-24). Jews are upset that Gentiles are invited, and Gentiles are insulted they are last to the table, as if second-class in God's kingdom. Stirring up controversy is the point of parables. Jesus models how to stir up the waters, also how to calm them (spoiler alert for Episode 8). To calm Philip, Little James cites Isaiah (42:1), reminding us that Gentiles would be "curious" about the Messiah. As to whether "highways and hedges" refer to Gentiles, Jesus (in the film) hedges by saying, "He who has ears to hear let him hear." He adds that the heart of *both* Jew and Gentile is "hard."

Were Gentiles in Jesus' line of ancestors?
Yes! Tamar, Rahab, and Ruth were Gentiles (Matthew 1:3-5), indicating that Jesus' ministry includes all ethnic groups, not just Israel.

What's with the tassels that Matthew ends up wearing on his robe?
Matthew at first refuses to take this precious religious item to settle an old man's huge tax liability. This old man (a shepherd) at one point says, "I am eager to meet my Maker, again." (In this film, this same character first met Jesus at the manger scene.) Matthew hides the prayer tassels as if they're forbidden by his new faith and gets angry when Mary Magdalene uncovers them. To Orthodox Jews, then and now, tassels ("tzitzit") on the four edges of their robe show obedience to Torah (Deuteronomy 22:12; Matthew 23:5). Matthew feels unworthy of tassels, even afraid of them, but makes peace with this throwback remnant, symbolic of his original Jewishness.

Is Gaius a secret believer?
He's getting closer, as is evident from his friendship with Simon and conversations about "the Jewish doctor" and "Shalom, Shalom"—the perfect peace that Gaius yearns for, and that Jesus represents.

What's with Peter appearing so weary and heavy-laden?

While many see him as "off" his game and make excuses for him, little do they know Peter is grieving the loss of a child in Eden's womb. John, understand Jesus' calling him to stay with someone in pain. John prefers strength in numbers. Instead, a softened heart is required. The ongoing tiff between John and Simon would be comical if it weren't so common. It's also sad, in that it shows the hurt and humanity of Simon and the obtuseness of guys trying to empathize. What galls Simon (and many of us) is that Jesus "could have prevented [the loss] but did not." John & Simon are among the many "weary and heavy-laden" invited to Jesus. He alone can carry the tough issues we lay on him (Matthew 11:28-30).

Was deafness (or blindness) regarded as a punishment for sin?
Yes, in the minds of many whom Jesus encountered (John 9:1-3), but he taught otherwise.

Who are these divisive groups that oppose Jesus and his followers?
Syrophoenicians and Nabataeans. A Syrophoenician hails from the borders of Tyre and Sidon, so a Canaanite (Matthew 15:21-22; Mark 7:26). The Nabataeans are considered descendants of Nebaioth, the firstborn of Ishmael, born of Abraham's union with Sarah's handmaid, Hagar (see Genesis 25:12-13), so commonly considered Arab people.

Drive it HOME Review & Respond: Worship, Journaling, Prayer

--. ?

--. ?

--. ?

Video Insights: What is the Gospel? -Melissa Dougherty

Type in URL: tinyurl.com/the-gospel-defined (20:24 min.)

Notes:

Video Insights: *What is the Gospel? –Melissa Dougherty*

Type in URL: tinyurl.com/the-gospel-defined (20:24 min.)

Notes:

Video Insights: *What is the Gospel? –Melissa Dougherty*

Type in URL: tinyurl.com/the-gospel-defined (20:24 min.)

Notes:

 **What is your favorite Chosen episode so far?**

NOTE FOR EVERYONE: Of course, there's a wide difference of opinion regarding the above question, but many pick this final episode. Regardless, because of its length, you might want to *first read over the passage on which the episode ends before beginning your study*: John 4:1-26 (see pages 111-113).

Sustenance (Episode 8A)

Study #9

INTRO: The cover on this guide illustrates the centrality of food for the hungry. But, of course, our hunger runs deeper than loaves and fish. We have a "God-shaped void" of spiritual hunger that only God himself can satisfy.

WATCH **View Episode 8A** *(3 min., from :00 to 3:22)* **> Discuss**

INTRO: Psalm 77, composed by Asaph in 990 B.C., provides the opening (and closing) of this episode.

1. As you reflect and review on this Season and this Psalm, how does one illustrate the other?

DISCOVER **Read Aloud > Mark It Up > Discuss**

INTRO: X

Look For:

In the Day of Trouble I Seek the Lord
To the choirmaster: according to Jeduthun. A Psalm of Asaph.
PSALM 77 I cry aloud to God,

aloud to God, and he will hear me.

² In the day of my trouble I seek the Lord;

in the night my hand is stretched out without wearying;

my soul refuses to be comforted.

³ When I remember God, I moan;

when I meditate, my spirit faints. *Selah*

⁴ You hold my eyelids open;

I am so troubled that I cannot speak.

⁵ I consider the days of old,

the years long ago.

[6] I said, "Let me remember my song in the night;

let me meditate in my heart."

Then my spirit made a diligent search:

[7] "Will the Lord spurn forever,

and never again be favorable?

[8] Has his steadfast love forever ceased?

Are his promises at an end for all time?

[9] Has God forgotten to be gracious?

Has he in anger shut up his compassion?" *Selah*

??????

WATCH **View Episode 8A Cont'd** (35 min., from 3:20 to 38:49) >

Discuss

INTRO: This season's Grand Finale focuses on feelings, food, and faith that God provides/cares for us in hard times. More healings, parables, and disputes among factions set up an epic climax that involves **Jesus** & Jews breaking bread with fractious Gentiles. Jesus affirms **Simon Peter** as essential for the success of this mission trip. Rabbi **Shmuel,** on his heresy hunt to arrest and eliminate Jesus, interviews witnesses.

1. *What people do you see here who are burdened in their soul, prime candidates for Jesus' message of "rest for the weary"?*

?. ??

DISCOVER *Read Aloud > Mark It Up > Discuss*

INTRO: X

Look For:

Jesus Feeds the Five Thousand

JOHN 6 After this Jesus went away to the other side of the Sea of Galilee, which is the Sea of Tiberias. ² And a large crowd was following him, because they saw the signs that he was doing on the sick. ³ Jesus went up on the mountain, and there he sat down with his disciples. ⁴ Now the Passover, the feast of the Jews, was at hand. ⁵ Lifting up his eyes, then, and seeing that a large crowd was coming toward him, Jesus said to Philip, "Where are we to buy bread, so that these people may eat?" ⁶ He said this to test him, for he himself knew what he would do. ⁷ Philip answered him, "Two hundred denarii worth of bread would not be enough for each of them to get a little."

⁸ One of his disciples, Andrew, Simon Peter's brother, said to him, ⁹ "There is a boy here who has five barley loaves and two fish, but what are they for so many?"

¹⁰ Jesus said, "Have the people sit down." Now there was much grass in the place. So the men sat down, about five thousand in number. ¹¹ Jesus then took the loaves, and when he had given thanks, he distributed them to those who were seated. So also the fish, as much as they wanted. ¹² And when they had eaten their fill, he told his disciples, "Gather up the leftover fragments, that nothing may be lost." ¹³ So they gathered them up and filled twelve baskets with fragments from the five barley loaves left by those who had eaten.

¹⁴ When the people saw the sign that he had done, they said, "This is indeed the Prophet who is to come into the world!"

I Am the Bread of Life
²⁵ When they found him on the other side of the sea, they said to him, "Rabbi, when did you come here?"

²⁶ Jesus answered them, "Truly, truly, I say to you, you are seeking me, not because you saw signs, but because you ate your fill of the loaves. ²⁷ Do not work for the food that perishes, but for the food that endures to eternal life, which the Son of Man will give to you. For on him God the Father has set his seal.". . .

³⁵ Jesus said to them, "I am the bread of life; whoever comes to me shall not hunger, and whoever believes in me shall never thirst. . . .

⁴¹ So the Jews grumbled about him, because he said, "I am the bread that came down from heaven."

⁴² They said, "Is not this Jesus, the son of Joseph, whose father and mother we know? How does he now say, 'I have come down from heaven'?"

⁴³ Jesus answered them, "Do not grumble among yourselves. ⁴⁴ No one can come to me unless the Father who sent me draws him. And I will raise him up on the last day.... ⁴⁷ Truly, truly, I say to you, whoever believes has eternal life. ⁴⁸ I am the bread of life. ⁴⁹ Your fathers ate the manna in the wilderness, and they died. ⁵⁰ This is the bread that comes down from heaven, so that one may eat of it and not die. ⁵¹ I am the living bread that came down from heaven. If anyone eats of this bread, he will live forever. And the bread that I will give for the life of the world is my flesh."

--. ?

--. ?

--. ?

RELATE   How It Applies to God / Life / You > Discuss

--. ?

--. ?

After watching > discovering > relating,
What slogan would you write or draw on your T-shirt?

Draft concepts:

Final design:

NOTES on Study #9 ~~Commentary and Historical~~ Context

Passage—Title

- ?

- ?

Passage—Title
- ?

- ?

Passage—Title
- ?

- ?

That's plausible but did it happen?

Question? Answer.

--. ?

--, ?

--, ?

Video Insights: What is the Gospel? -Melissa Dougherty
Type in URL: tinyurl.com/the-gospel-defined (20:24 min.)
Notes:

Video Insights: *What is the Gospel? –Melissa Dougherty*
Type in URL: tinyurl.com/the-gospel-defined (20:24 min.)
Notes:

_____

Video Insights: *What is the Gospel? –Melissa Dougherty*
Type in URL: tinyurl.com/the-gospel-defined (20:24 min.)
Notes:

_____

Time to put it all together

–The tenth meeting includes a review of Season One, a bridge to Season Two, and reflection on what we've learned and experienced so far.

Note: For this gathering, your group could meet at your normal time, or as an alternative, you could plan to meet in a special place for a longer event which can do wonders as a group bonding experience. Pages 127-132 can be used for an *extended Drive it HOME* session, or for an *Day-Long* event *or Weekend retreat.*

See page 16 for an overview of a **Day-Long Event** or **Weekend Retreat.** See jesusstudy.org for further suggestions under *Leaders*.

It is a priority to have as many in your group come as possible, hopefully everyone, no matter what you do! So, discuss options and get it on your group members' schedules, as early as possible.

Hopefully, you and your group will continue the Chosen experience and invite new people to your next study!

Rest for
the Weary (Episode 8B)

Study #10

INTRO:

. To convince us we need more tha food, Jesus tells stories (parables) of the Kingdom. Jesus embraces the apostles, especially **Simon** ("I'm sorry. Don't let me go, please!"), Jesus is all inclusive in his embrace of fractious Gentiles and enemies within the council of Pharisees (**Rabbi Shmuel**), whose hearts are softening.

????????

WATCH **View Ep. 8B** (34 min., *from 41:56 to 112:38*) **> Discuss**

INTRO: Rabbi **Shmuel** seems to renounce his heresy hunt to pray with Jesus. "Come to me all you who labor and are heavy-laden" is Jesus' call after giving us all we can carry. **Jesus** walks on water and embraces risk-taking, grief-stricken **Peter**.

1. *What do you find most risky about Jesus and Peter on the water?*

2. *Even if you are a risk-averse person, what do you find most relevant in this walking on water incident?*

3. *Do ou think Shmuel ended up praying with Jesus? Why or why not?*

?. *??*

DISCOVER **Read Aloud > Mark It Up > Discuss**

INTRO: The disciples, having gone to town to find food, now return and offer some to Jesus. His response leaves them even more confused. Apparently, he is getting his hunger satisfied with something else, and he wants them to have the same experience.

Look For:

Jesus Feeds the Four Thousand

MARK 8 In those days, when again a great crowd had gathered, and they had nothing to eat, he called his disciples to him and said to them, ² "I have compassion on the crowd, because they have been with me now three days and have nothing to eat. ³ And if I send them away hungry to their homes, they will faint on the way. And some of them have come from far away." ⁴ And his disciples answered him, "How can one feed these people with bread here in this desolate place?" ⁵ And he asked them, "How many loaves do you have?" They said, "Seven." ⁶ And he directed the crowd to sit down on the ground. And he took the seven loaves, and having given thanks, he broke them and gave them to his disciples to set before the people; and they set them before the crowd. ⁷ And they had a few small fish. And having blessed them, he said that these also should be set before them. ⁸ And they ate and were satisfied. And they took up the broken pieces left over, seven baskets full. ⁹ And there were about four thousand people. And he sent them away. ¹⁰ And immediately he got into the boat with his disciples and went to the district of Dalmanutha.

Jesus Walks on the Water

MATTHEW ²² Immediately Jesus made the disciples get into the boat and go on ahead of him to the other side, while he dismissed the crowd. ²³ After he had dismissed them, he went up on a mountainside by himself to pray. Later that night, he was there alone, ²⁴ and the boat was already a considerable distance from land, buffeted by the waves because the wind was against it.

25 Shortly before dawn Jesus went out to them, walking on the lake. 26 When the disciples saw him walking on the lake, they were terrified. "It's a ghost," they said, and cried out in fear.

27 But Jesus immediately said to them: "Take courage! It is I. Don't be afraid."

28 "Lord, if it's you," Peter replied, "tell me to come to you on the water."

29 "Come," he said.

Then Peter got down out of the boat, walked on the water and came toward Jesus. 30 But when he saw the wind, he was afraid and, beginning to sink, cried out, "Lord, save me!"

31 Immediately Jesus reached out his hand and caught him. "You of little faith," he said, "why did you doubt?"

32 And when they climbed into the boat, the wind died down. 33 Then those who were in the boat worshiped him, saying, "Truly you are the Son of God."

34 When they had crossed over, they landed at Gennesaret.

?????????

View Ep. 8B Cont'd (3 min., from 112:38 to 15.40) >

Discuss

INTRO: The psalmist Asaph is presenting (in this film, fore and aft) his new song to King David and his wife. This prescient psalm anticipates the sorrows of **Simon & Eden**, also of **John the Baptist** (his cameo appearance at the end is a spoiler alert for Season Four). Psalm 77 is fittingly read (and illustrated), then and now.

1. What is the significance of the film synchronizing the experiences of Simon and Eden, both immersed in water and in over their heads?

?. ??

?. ??

A Psalm of Asaph (Psalm 77:10-19, cont'd from 77:1-9 on page ???)

PSALM 77 ¹⁰ Then I said, "I will appeal to this,

to the years of the right hand of the Most High."

¹¹ I will remember the deeds of the Lord;

yes, I will remember your wonders of old.

¹² I will ponder all your work,

and meditate on your mighty deeds.

¹³ Your way, O God, is holy.

What god is great like our God?

¹⁴ You are the God who works wonders;

you have made known your might among the peoples.

¹⁵ You with your arm redeemed your people,

the children of Jacob and Joseph. *Selah*

¹⁶ When the waters saw you, O God,

when the waters saw you, they were afraid;

indeed, the deep trembled.

¹⁷ The clouds poured out water;

the skies gave forth thunder;

your arrows flashed on every side.

¹⁸ The crash of your thunder was in the whirlwind;

your lightnings lighted up the world;

the earth trembled and shook.

¹⁹ Your way was through the sea,

your path through the great waters;

yet your footprints were unseen.

--. ?

--. ?

--. ?

RELATE **How It Applies to God / Life / You > Discuss**

--. ?

--. ?

--. ?

After watching > discovering > relating,
What slogan would you write or draw on your T-shirt?

Draft concepts:

Final design:

NOTES on Study #10 Commentary and Historical Context

PASSAGE—Title

-

-

PASSAGE—Title

-

-

PASSAGE—Title

-

-

-

 **That's plausible but did it happen?**

In what sense did the "success" (of this mission trip) depend on Simon?

While viewers are naturally drawn to Eden's pain, Scripture doesn't focus on her but on Peter. So, the film sets us up for a transformational moment in his life. He's so distracted and distraught ("I was a mistake"), that no one can imagine him as a leader. Little did they know that it would be Simon's entrepreneurial, risk-taking spirit that snags a boat to get home and shows one and all the faith that transforms ("I'm sorry. Don't let me go, please!").

What about the Good News caused the hostility among Gentile groups?

The beautiful Nabataean, Fatiyah, complains that construction business is down because the town's *augur* was "poisoned" (converted)! An "augur" is a soothsayer who reads various "signs" (a bird's flight, lightning strike, or chicken's innards) to see if a project was beginning on a good omen or not. When the augur from Abila turned to Jesus, no one had the guts to begin construction or any other project without knowing if it was approved by the gods or not. Eremis from Athens is likewise thwarted; he too reads the "auspices" of pagan gods for good omens before relocating his bronze-casting business. Economic reasons are driving people away/toward Jesus. Such pagan groups fight each other and the Pharisees (Machir, in this film). Moderating Jews (Leander, from Episode 6) seek peace and clarity.

Was Jesus' message to the thousands relayed as shown in the film?

Humans were the only megaphone/telephone/speaker system in that era. We are not to be passive listeners only, but doers and conveyors of the Word, as were the Twelve (quite literally echoing Jesus in this film).

Did feeding of the masses happen as shown in the film?

The film merges into one mass feeding what Scripture distinguishes as two events. In "feeding the 5000" (Matthew 14:13-21), Jesus fed mostly Jews with "five loaves and two fish"—brought by a boy (Telemachus, in the film, who debuted in Episode 7). That boy's lunch was multiplied in "12 baskets" brought by 12 apostles. Such details contrast with "feeding the 4000" (15:32-39), where "seven loaves" and "seven baskets" fed diverse Gentiles, depicted in the film as hostile groups from the Decapolis. Jesus defuses their hostility with meekness, his miraculous healing of those coming from afar (15:29-31), by listening to differences and telling parables (of Sower, Mustard Seed, and Hidden Treasure—all in Matthew 13). Jesus' show-and-tell-and-conceal style enables good soil/hearts to receive the seed/gospel to sell all and buy-in, to hunger for more and be satisfied. The film shows men, women & kids eating together—contrary to the standards of that day.

Rabbi Shmuel doesn't have his heart in the witch-hunt for Jesus. Why?
The film shows in 3D a more complete picture of diverse Jewish leaders, who were not uniformly opposed to Jesus for breaking bread with Gentiles. Leander speaks for many: "We've hurt each other, but Jesus is healing us!" Rabbi Schmuel separates from the other Pharisees and seeks comfort and counsel from Jesus. Jesus invites the rabbi to pray with him about letting go of old ways. Did he or not? Matthew asserts that Jesus prayed alone on that occasion (14:23).

Drive it HOME Review & Respond: Worship, Journaling, Prayer

--. ?

--. ?

--. ?

Video Insights: Woman at the Well   -Olivia Lane
Type in URL: tinyurl.com/woman-at-the-well-song (4:39 min.)

Notes: Other Videos:

_____

Video Insights: Woman at the Well   -Olivia Lane
Type in URL: tinyurl.com/woman-at-the-well-song (4:39 min.)
Notes: Other Videos:

_____

Video Insights: What is the Gospel? -Melissa Dougherty
Type in URL: tinyurl.com/the-gospel-defined (20:24 min.)
Notes:

_____

Your Faith Journey

-For an Extended Drive it HOME Session, or

-A Drive it HOME Day-Long Event, or

-A Drive it HOME Weekend Retreat

The next four pages provide a *look back* on your experience with the study. They can be used for an extended time of home reflection or as the outline of a longer gathering (see page 15.). For more input on organizing these gatherings, access the website under *Leaders*.

Such longer gatherings provide a time to go deeper as well as a great bonding opportunity within your group. The goal is to build friend-ships and momentum in prayer, and preparation to continue reaching out and enfolding others into the story of Jesus.

What are your "big picture" takeaways from your study:

What are your best takeaways from each study?

Study #1, Beyond Mountains / Homecoming, E 8B/E 1A
(pp. 21-34): Genesis 1:1-5; John 1:1-14

Study #2, Homecoming, Episode 1B (pp. 35-44):
Luke 10:25-37; Luke 15:1-7

Study #3, Two by Two, Episode 2 (pp. 45-54):
Psalm 13; John 1:43-51

Study #4, Physician, Heal Yourself, Episode 3 (pp. 55-64):
Matthew 4:23-25; Philippians 2:1-18

Study #5, Clean, Part 1, Episode 4 (pp. 65-74):
John 5:1-15

More takeaways?

Study #6, Clean, Pt 2, *Episode 5* (pp. 75-84)

   Mark 1:1-8, 14-15; Mark 5:1-20

Study #7, Intensity in Tent City, *Episode 6 (pp. 85-94):*

   1 Sam 21:1-6; Mark 2:23-3:6; Rom 8:1-2, 31-39

Study #8, Ears to Hear, *Episode 7 (pp 95-104):*

   John 14:15-21, 25-27; Luke 11:1-13

Study #9, Sustenance, *Episode 8A (pp. 105-116):*

   Psalm 139

Study #10, For Those Who are Heavy Ladened, *Episode 8B*

   (pp 117-126): Matthew 5:1-12

Read this definition of faith and "Mark It Up!"

The Chosen is meant to take you into the eyes and ears of the people who followed Jesus. We believe that if you can see Jesus through the eyes of those who met him, you can be changed and impacted in the same way they were.... If we can connect you with their burdens and struggles and questions, then ideally, we can connect you to the solution, to the answer to those questions. —Dallas Jenkins

One definition of genuine faith is *giving all you know about yourself to all you know about God.* Such is the call to humility. The more you hang around Jesus, the more you realize that he isn't impressed with pretension. Maybe that's why he—the Servant-King, God's under-stated Messiah—made no grand entry. Instead, Jesus shows up as a baby, born in a dirty stable to a peasant girl, in a nondescript town.

30 years later, for three short years, he announces that the Kingdom of God has arrived, complete with spiritually intriguing stories and miracles. He offers forgiveness of sin, and reconciliation to God the Father—all culminating in his crucifixion, resurrection, and ascension.

Something is going on here. No one could make this stuff up. If noth-ing more, **the story of Jesus is the most [_____ fill in the blank] story that humanity has to offer**. The Gospel writers certainly felt this way and their eagerness to describe this off-the-charts, unusual *eternity-meets-time event* pours through their accounts.

From your study, **write in the adjective** *that best describes Jesus' story:*
>   *Remarkable...*
>   *Compelling...*
>   *Audacious...*
>   *Captivating...*
>   *Fascinating...*

No fair picking them all!   *Intriguing...*
We chose one—what's yours?   *Other...*
Share why you selected it with your group.

Watch > Discover > Relate the Most _____ Story Ever Told.

Do you increasingly find yourself caught up in Jesus' story, as well? Do you want it, and him, to influence your life more deeply? Then, take on what you learn. If Jesus says to love your enemies, try it out. Or, if he says to show hospitality like the Good Samaritan, or to help find lost sheep like a Good Shepherd, then do it.

As you "try on Jesus' teaching," you will find it not only making sense, but that you will also need to look to him for the wisdom, strength, and courage to take the risk of making some hard choices. Thankfully, in this journey of faith, his forgiveness is always close at hand.

1. *How have you connected with the above quote by Dallas?*

2. *How do you respond to the definition of faith given on page 129?*

3. *Which teaching of Jesus would God have you "try on" right now?*

4. *With whom can you share what you've learned and its impact on you?*

Faith Journey Notes:

Background Notes Where his story came from

Early tradition identifies Matthew, Mark, Luke, and John as the ones who introduced Jesus to the First Century world and to ours. Their portrait of him is both historically unique and remarkably consistent.

MATTHEW: Given his occupation as a tax collector for the Roman government, we can only imagine the initial tension between Matthew (also called Levi) and the other disciples. But reconciliation lay at the heart of Jesus' message (see *The Sermon on the Mount,* Mathew 5-7). Matthew's Gospel emphasizes the interconnectedness between the Old and New Testaments and provides young believers a systematic tutorial on Jesus' teaching.

MARK: This Gospel has been generally recognized as the account coming from Peter. Mark begins his first "sentence" with no verb: *The beginning of the Gospel about Jesus Christ, the Son of God.* His last sentence ends with the women fleeing Jesus' empty tomb *because they were afraid.* For Mark, Jesus is a man of action. To help believers facing persecution from the Roman state, Mark focuses on Jesus as the Suffering Servant who "came to serve" (Mark 10:45).

LUKE: An educated Greek physician and traveling companion of Paul, Luke authored the book of Acts and the Gospel that bears his name. Although Luke never met Jesus himself, he had a close relationship with Paul, and was acquainted with most of the key eyewitnesses who knew Jesus (Luke 1:1-4). After extensive interviews with these contacts, Luke begins: "Since I myself have carefully investigated everything from the beginning, it seemed good also to me to write an orderly account" (Luke 1:3).

JOHN: A fisherman and brother of James, he writes, "In the beginning was the Word," offering a rather obvious parallel to the opening words of Genesis. In the "first Genesis," God spoke *Creation* into existence, and in the "second Genesis" God speaks *Redemption* into existence: "The Word became flesh and made his dwelling among us" (1:14). This "Word made flesh" is who John wants his readers to know.

Knowing those who knew him best

Mary Magdalene: One of several women mentioned in Luke 8:2-3 who had been "cured of evil spirits and diseases" and was following Jesus. Having been delivered from seven demons, she is with Jesus at the cross and is the first one to whom Jesus appears after the Crucifixion (Luke 8:2-3; John 19:25-27; John 20:1-18).

John the Baptist: Miraculously conceived shortly before his cousin Jesus, he heralds Jesus, as foretold by Isaiah (40:3-5), calling Jews to repent in preparation for the Messiah. After baptizing Jesus, he is imprisoned and later beheaded for the threat he posed to Herod Antipas. Jesus identifies him as *the greatest of those born of women* (John 1:6-34; Matthew 3:1-17; 11:1-19; 14:1-12; Luke 1:5-25, 57-80).

Andrew: One of the first to follow Jesus, he brings his brother, Simon (Peter). Together with fellow fishermen, James and John, Andrew leaves everything to follow Jesus after the miraculous catch. He also plays a key role in the feeding of the 5,000 (John 1:40-42; 6:8-9).

Simon: This fisherman meets Jesus and is later renamed Peter, *the Rock.* Brought to Jesus by his brother, Andrew, he is well-known for walking (and sinking) on water, slicing off a soldier's ear, denying Jesus before his death, being a prominent leader in the early Christian movement, and for writing 1 and 2 Peter (Matthew 14:25-32; 16:13-28; Mark 14:66-72; John 1:40-42; Luke 5:1-11).

James and John: With Simon, they become Jesus' closest disciples. Appropriately nicknamed by Jesus as the "sons of thunder" (Luke 9:54), they were Simon's partners and, like him, they left everything to follow Jesus after the catch of fish (Mark 3:17; Luke 5:1-11). John goes on to write a Gospel, three letters, and the Book of Revelation.

Matthew: Also known as Levi, is a despised tax collector when Jesus calls him from his tax booth to follow Him. He *left everything and followed him,* and invites many friends and coworkers to a dinner with Jesus (Luke 5:27-32). He authors the Gospel of Matthew.

James the Less (*micros,* meaning "little" or "young") and **Thaddeus**: Two lesser-known disciples: "Little James," a son of Alphaeus (Mark

3:18), could have been Matthew's brother (also a son of Alphaeus, Mark 2:14), but is never identified as such. Thaddeus, aka Jude/Judas, may have gotten his nickname to distinguish him from the other Judas thus avoiding negative connotations.

Thomas (aka Didymus, or "twin"): Best known for doubting: *Unless I see the nail marks in his hands… I will not believe* (John 20:25). Thomas could, maybe more accurately, be called *logical*. Regardless, we see a whole-hearted passion, even an openness to die with Jesus (11:16), and fear of missing him (14:5). Thomas, the last of The Twelve to see Jesus after the resurrection, upon seeing him proclaims, *My Lord and my God* (20:24-29).

Mary, mother of Jesus: She is the teenager God chose to give birth to Jesus, who was conceived in her by the Holy Spirit. She raises Jesus with **Joseph,** who married her after an angel appears to him in a dream, and who probably died before Jesus began his adult ministry. She weeps at the Crucifixion, witnesses the resurrected Christ, and, along with at least some of her other children (Acts 1:14), is part of the early church (Luke 1:26-56; 2:5-7; 8:19-21; John 2:1-12; 19:25-27).

Philip is a disciple of John the Baptist, and a friend of Andrew. He changes allegiance from John to Jesus, and seeks out a friend, **Nathanael,** who wonders aloud, "Can anything good come out of Nazareth?" Philp seemingly quotes Jesus, "Come and see!" Nathanael does and is amazed that Jesus "met him" before they meet: "Before Philip called you, when you were under the fig tree, I saw you."

Simon (the Zealot: We don't know a lot about him from the gospel record other than his association with the Zealots, a group of Jewish insurrectionists who opposed Roman rule. Without much to go on, there has been a wide variety of speculation. Some options are: the same person as Simeon of Jerusalem who became an early Christian leader, Simon, the brother of Jesus or perhaps a cousin of Jesus.

Judas (Iscariot)—was a name probably given to him as a designation of his native place, Kerioth, a town in Judah. In *The Chosen* he is introduced as the last of the disciples to join, but the New Testament only indicates that he was one of the Twelve, not when he joined.

Spoiler Alert! What happens next . .

Episode 1: *Season Four is coming!*

Episode 2:

Episode 3:

Episode 4:

Episode 5:

Episode 6:

Episode 7:

Episode 8:

Mark where it happened on the map

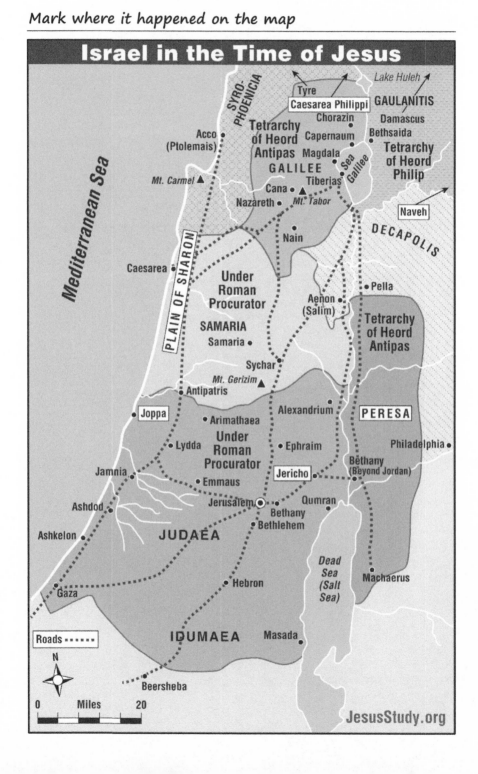

Record locations cited and what happened there:

– Bethlehem Ephrathah: Micah 5:2 (p. 22) Jesus' birthplace

– Nazareth, Jesus' hometown: Luke 2:4 (p. 26)

– Bethlehem (City of David): Luke 2:4, 15 (p. 26-27)

–

–

–

–

–

–

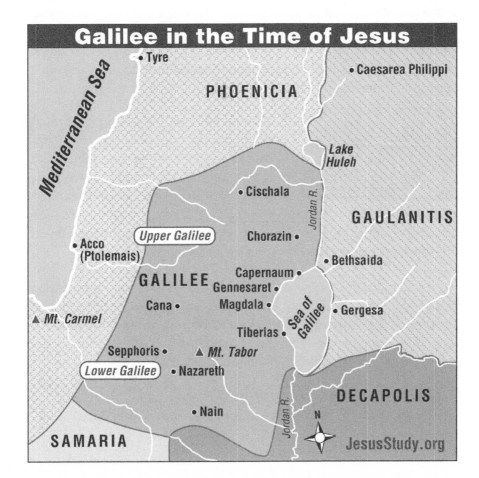

Can you trust The Chosen?

Some have raised questions about the authenticity of *The Chosen*—which is what this guide's *Realistic But Real?* sections highlight. An analogy to Bible translation could be made in this regard.

Some Bible translations strictly follow the original Hebrew and Greek, but such very literal renditions can make it difficult to read in other languages. Other translations focus on meaning by reworking sentence structures into a better, native-reading format: a "dynamic equivalent." (*The Chosen Study* uses one slightly tilted toward literal: ESV.)

Still other "translations" paraphrase the original words, or even add interpretation, thus amplifying (but not contradicting) the meaning.

Every film enactment of biblical events falls somewhere on a similar spectrum: from a literal (word-for-word) depiction, to a dynamic equivalent, to a non-literal paraphrase. In the case of *The Chosen*, it would be fair to characterize it as beyond paraphrase to an "amplified version." Some would use this byline under it: *Based on a True Story*.

Such "non-literal," *historical fiction* relies on artistic license, and can cause discomfort which is understandable. If that is true for you, check out the videos by Dallas entitled: *Can you trust The Chosen?* (tinyurl.com/trusting-the-chosen), as well as an interview with Jonathan Roumie, (tinyurl.com/roumie-interview), who portrays Jesus. These videos convey their perspective and may prove helpful.

We regularly point out what happened versus plausible speculation from *The Chosen*. Ultimately, *The Chosen* is a TV show, and the Bible is the only media inspired by God, given to inform us of the truth and the way things happened. Film brings supportive context and three-dimensional color to the two-dimensional writing on the page.

Dallas' heartfelt, well-conceived mission (see page 17) is why we vigorously support *The Chosen* and have developed *The Chosen Study*.

Background Notes:

Bible apps, online access and a NT Journal

 The **You Version** app, installed on over 500M devices, is used on smartphones and tablets, and accessed online at bible.com and youversion.com. Excellent for reading.

 Bible Gateway is a searchable online Bible in 200 versions and 70 languages, that can be read and referenced online at biblegateway.com. Excellent for researching.

 BibleProject.com and its app, used in some studies, include a quality collection of videos on books of the Bible, biblical themes, and word studies. Excellent for learning.

Journaling New Testament

Apply the *Mark-It-Up* study method to the entire New Testament with this modestly priced, double-spaced format for study and note taking.

To find out more about this NT: tinyurl.com/nt-journal

More Notes:

Leader's Notes

The Chosen Vision: Dallas and his team share the goal of *reaching a billion people with the message of Jesus.* Our "loaves and fish" effort joins their far-reaching aspirations by **helping study leaders** facilitate **discussions about Jesus with everyone we know, and to see people grow into and as Christ followers.**

If you're on the fence about leading, consider Jesus' challenge to Andrew in Episode 8 of Season One about traveling through the hated Samaritan territory, a place considered unclean and dangerous: *Did you join me for safety reasons?*

So, you're interested in leading a Chosen Study? Here's what to do:

Gather a Core Team

 The Chosen Study Team
is a small group with a big purpose.
Draw together a core group made up of those who have seen something "different" in Jesus and want others to experience that difference. The team meets together regularly (shoot for weekly) to support the group process and pray. They plan, oversee the food, and invite friends and family to join in. This team can take on the following roles:

–***The Group Leader*** oversees the group's study and discussion process and seeks to foster one-on-one friendship evangelism and discipleship within the group. We encourage the Group Leader to model servant/leadership within the group and to send out weekly emails.

–***The Prayer Team Promoter*** finds ways to support the Study in prayer.

–***The Meal Organizer*** oversees the food. See *Resources* at the website for theme potluck sign-up sheets. Meal Organizers can also keep in touch during the week with group emails. (The first meal will likely be something like a pizza instead of a planned potluck.)

–**Child Care Helper** for younger families who need such help to come.

–**Set-Up/Sign-Up/Name Tag/Greeter** should be designated, especially for larger groups. For the people who may not feel comfortable at first, you'll want to extend hospitality and friendship from the start.

–**"Tech Person"** to oversee film management—stopping and starting.

–**Small Group Facilitators** (for larger studies—eight or more) oversee their group. **It is best to sit around small tables with just four to six others** (and best to separate spouses), rotating members weekly.

–**Day-Long or Weekend Event Organizer** (see page 15 and the website).

FYI: There are two series. **The Chosen Series** that follows *The Chosen* and **The Bible Series** which includes other film and passage selections from the Gospels and various books of Scripture. (See pages 156-157 and the website for these options.)

Be Inclusive of Everyone

Who to invite? Everyone who is open to come: The religious, the skeptics, the non-religious, the seekers—you name it. This is to be a fun, interactive place that values and respects everyone.

We hope group members share differences of opinion and viewpoints from all over the spiritual map. We're glad for that. Each person brings their own background. We're not here to judge. We love to stir up discussion and hear unaccustomed perspectives. As Jesus said to Simon in episode seven: *Get used to different!*

Sharing and Prayer: To respect where people are spiritually, encourage believers to **avoid insider-type sharing**—which can characterize typical Bible study groups. (Also, prayer should primarily take place before you come/after you leave, not during group time.) A Chosen Study is a **skeptic- and seeker-friendly outreach group** for mutual learning, and to develop deeper friendships both inside and outside the group context.

Get the Word Out

Direct Invitation: Yes, we still do that, right?! Indeed, it is by far the most effective means.

Email Invitation: Get the word out quickly by sending a link to the trailer, website, and a flyer attachment.

Text Invitation: Send out a photo, or better yet, a digital photo (JPG) of your flyer, and an active link to the trailer and website.

Flyers: Contact us at our website to receive sample flyers in MS Word that you can adapt and print or make up your own to hand out.

Create a Facebook Event and **Church Announcements** to the masses.

Plan for Food

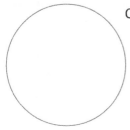

Our studies seek to connect us to God AND to each other. What better way to bring people together than by sharing food and conversa-tion? We encourage starting with a meal, potluck or, at least, finger food. The role of overseeing the meals is a tremendous service to the group.

Lead/Facilitate the Group

You can begin small—with just one friend, one-on-one, or gather a group. Pray, invite, read, and underline the key points on pages 8-15 and 143-150. The leader's notes integrated along the way are for both current and future leaders to gain confidence in how to facilitate their groups.

Multiply Your Efforts—through small/large (8+) group combos

Combing small groups within a larger group:
When a group starts large or grows larger—*to eight or more*—the larger size presents unique opportunities. Small groups provide a *depth* of intimacy which allows members to participate more. Larger group interaction can then draw out the very best insights from the small group discussions to offer a *breadth* of give-and-take sharing.

Day-Long or Weekend Event Organizer (see page 15 and the website).

This combination **provides for two (shorter) discussion times**, with the best of both dynamics, and gives group leaders the role of a "dialogical" (two-way), not "monological" (one-way), teacher. After each small group time, the leader brings together the larger group for a "check-in" to highlight what was discussed within the small groups.

A small/large group combination **offers a chance for the core team to facilitate the smaller groups**. The goal is to foster a guided conversation. This, likewise, is true for a large group leader on a larger scale. Quality, dialogical teaching brings a soft touch to the group sharing, by focusing on the best insights gleaned from the small groups.

Larger groups thus **provide discipleship opportunities** for group members to step into the role of small group facilitators, as part of the core Chosen Study team. The goal is to help equip an increasing number of these leaders to multiply their outreach efforts in the lives of others. The challenge during the group time is to keep up the pace.

If you're currently a group member with such aspirations, feel free to study through the guide notes, go through the website and look for an opportunity to join a team, or to start your own Chosen Study!

For Leader Support: jesusstudy.org/contact

The website's primary purpose is to equip current and future leaders to make disciples and provide a community of discipleship for those using *The Chosen* for outreach and growth. *How can we serve you?*

Eight Group Ground Rules to Enhance Your Experience

1. *The Leader* is a **facilitator** of discussion, guiding the group through questions rather than statements. He or she is responsible to **prepare for and oversee group interaction** and to **help with outreach**.

2. *The Guide* makes for a valuable personal study but is especially set up to help **current and future leaders** facilitate watching, study, and discussion in one-to-one, and in small/large group settings.

3. *Prior Preparation* is not expected. We do, however, have a **Drive it HOME** reflection time and **Video Insights** for post-Study follow-up.

4. *Each Group Member* "owns the group," and is thus seen as a key contributor of comments and questions. **Talkative members** should defer to others and **quiet members**, speak out. *The conversation engagement around the circle should look like a pinball machine!*

5. *Group Focus* is controlled by its purpose. *The Chosen* Study allows the episode and Scripture passage to **govern the discussion**, rather than Bible commentaries or cross referencing. Tangents are to be avoided or at least "tabled," until after the group meeting is over.

6. *Personal Growth* from studying Jesus is our goal. Such growth naturally includes a **focus on humility** and **child-like faith**.

7. *Group Growth* happens as **friendships form and deepen**. Members should see themselves as more than just a study group, but as a community where consistency, accountability, self-disclosure, empathy, and reaching out to others are key characteristics.

8. *Avoid making "guest appearances."* Don't let *stay-at-home feelings* or distractions dictate whether you come. **Commit to attend** every meeting. Take this gathering seriously—for you and for others.

Fight "those feelings" and the distractions by <u>signing this challenge</u>:

Unless out-of-town or near death's door, I'll be there: _____

Grit your teeth and go for it! Your name here.

Eight Don'ts of Leading Group Discussions

You're NOT a teacher, you're *a **facilitator***. To lead a highly productive group discussion, start with what NOT to do and you're halfway there!

1. **Don't answer your own questions.** Otherwise, the group will look to you as "the teacher" rather than "the facilitator." You're not just the questioner. You should participate like any member, but don't be the first one to answer your own question.

2. **Don't over-talk.** Groups with an overtalkative leader will often sit back—in boredom! 90% of what we hear we forget, but 90% of what we say, we remember. So, your goal is to get your group talking. Get them remembering. Get them learning.

3. **Don't be afraid of silence.** Silence may mean you need to rephrase the question, but if you "bail out your group" when silent, you set a bad precedent. To exercise patience, count in your head from 100 to 0 before answering—then, only if you must. Oh, yes, they'll talk!

4. **Don't be content with just one answer.** For every written question feel free to ask a follow-up question or two, like: "Does anyone else have a thought?" This allows several people to respond.

5. **Don't expect group members to respond with an answer each time.** They'll be tempted to look straight at you solely, especially when the group is new. Instead, you want them talking to each other, so you don't have to be the "discussion hub" (see page 150).

6. **Don't reject an answer as wrong.** Respond to questionable answers by asking, "How did you come to that conclusion?" or "There's probably a difference of opinion here. Does anyone else have another way of looking at this?" Be affirming to everyone.

7. **Don't be afraid of controversy.** Different opinions are a good thing.

8. **Don't allow the group to end late.** If the discussion proves fruitful, end on time. Don't let the group drag on, but for those who choose to stay, give opportunity to discuss the issue in more depth.

Eight Do's of Leading Group Discussions

You don't need to be an expert or trained teacher to lead a discussion group. Your role is that of a **facilitator**, one who guides others into a productive conversation centering on key points of the film clips and Bible studies. It's an honor to be able to serve your group in this way.

1. **Bring along your own curiosity and have fun with it.** Good start!

2. **Pace the study.** It's the leader's responsibility to both start and end on time. Keep up a flexible pace with one eye on the clock and the other on the content. There may be more questions than you have time for; so, if necessary, skip some questions. Press ahead!

3. **Give members the chance to study on their own.** They are free to do so—or not. There is no expectation of prior preparation.

4. **Have the Scripture read aloud.** Ask a group member to read. Some feel uncomfortable doing so in public, so don't make a surprise assignment unless you know they are willing and are good at it.

5. **Be on the alert for overtalkative people.** Someone who over-talks can squeeze the life out of a group. If this is a problem, engage with that group member after the meeting, and enlist their help to join you in your goal to get everyone involved in the discussion.

6. **Involve everyone, more or less equally.** Sit across from quiet people to draw them out, and next to talkative people to make less eye contact. If helpful, go around the circle with a question.

7. **Keep the discussion on track by avoiding tangents.** Tangents may seem important but can hurt purposeful discussion, leading the group to talk about less important things. "Important tangents" provide opportunities for conversation outside the group's time.

8. **Conduct a discussion first with general, then specific questions.** Your goal in NOT to get into one-and-done responses; rather, your goal is to start an engaging dialogue with several people responding to a particular question in a back-and-forth way (see next page).

Facilitating Group Interaction: Monological vs. Dialogical

If tables (small round or rectangle) are available, they are preferred for the meals and for group study (of ideally four to six participants each).

Dialogical interaction engages wide-ranging participation. Such give-and-take discussion sparked by the *table leader* and the *up-front leader* is desired. **Interaction from a leader's question is visualized below:**

Inferior Monological Interaction   *Superior Dialogical Interaction*

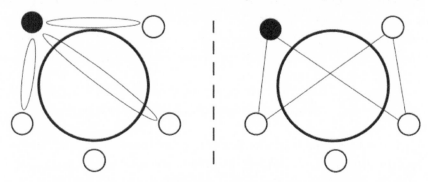

Small/Larger Group Combination—Can Work with Eight or More

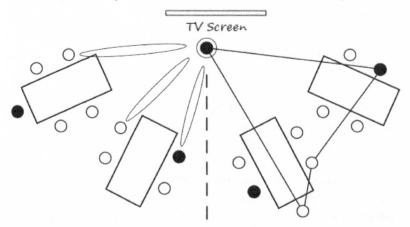

TV Screen

Dialogical leading *facilitates interaction* among your group members and prevents you from "brokering" the participants' comments with your own or monopolizing the discussion as seen above. As a leader you can participate, but your goal is to get others talking. **Remember:** 90% of what you say they'll forget, but 90% of what you get them to say, they'll remember! So, get them get them talking and learning!!

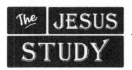 Have you seen something different in Jesus?

Join a Jesus Study Team and consider becoming a

Jesus Study Leader

Leader's Notes: What applies most to you and your group?

-

-

-

-

-

-

-

-

-

-

-

-

-

-

-

Your Chosen Group: Names, info., prayer concerns, etc.

-

-

-

-

-

-

-

-

-

-

-

-

-

-

-

-

Your Chosen Group: Names, info., prayer concerns, etc.

–

–

–

–

–

–

–

–

–

–

–

–

–

–

–

Note: For a sign-up sheet to print off, see the website under *Resources*.

Leader's Notes: